I Started Out
as a
Middle Child

The True Story
of a
~~Fairly~~ ~~Really~~ ~~Awfully~~ Nice Person

Written by Jonnie Garstka
Illustrated by Karin Tyndall

Riverhaven Books

I Started Out as a Middle Child is a collection of the author's memories and recollections. It is all true…unless you ask her family….

Copyright© 2019 by Jonnie Garstka

Published in the United States by Riverhaven Books, Massachusetts.

ISBN: 978-1-937588-99-1

Printed in the United States of America
by Country Press, Lakeville, Massachusetts

Edited by Riverhaven Books
Designed by Stephanie Lynn Blackman
Whitman, MA

Dedications

To Paul:

Thank you for always telling me to "Go for it!"

To Sandie:

When you left us, Gundi became the sole middle child instead
of a collective one with me. Now she's being a pain.

To Lili:

When your Grandma Sandie died, we asked you, "What do
you think happens when a person dies?"
Your answer, that you think a person becomes a flower, has
given our family great joy. Thank you.

Introduction

I hereby dedicate the following series of anecdotes, family misinformation, and gross exaggerations to you, my terrific children, whose high school years were ruined (or so you said) by your friends' reactions to these newspaper columns. A reminiscence of my life in a large family, they list all my siblings' faults and blames them and my parents for everything that ever went wrong in my life. You should know I love my parents and brothers and sisters very much. It's just a lot of fun taking pokes at them now and then.

Pay attention to the heart of each story, because if you smile and feel happy after reading one, that's probably how I felt while writing it.

Home Sweet Home

The house I grew up in had to be the perfect place to raise a large family. Situated in rural Connecticut, it was surrounded by apple trees, hay fields, and small ponds.

We were told it was originally planned to be a car dealership, but its location was too far from town. It had ten bedrooms (offices) and five bathrooms (more offices). The living room alone measured 54' by 40'. The floors were marbleized concrete; the walls stone. At times we literally, and figuratively, climbed them.

The furniture, like the house, was outsized and overstated. There was a fourteen-foot long oak dining table and a huge oriental rug my dad bought at the demise of one of the brownstones in Manhattan.

My mom's concert grand piano was set in a corner of the living room next to the six-foot high opening in the stone fireplace we could, and sometimes did, walk into. On cold winter nights there'd be a fire and we'd lie near the hearth and listen while my mom played everything from Gershwin to Beethoven. In the spring there would be pretend weddings with apple blossom crowns and scowling grooms.

My childhood was noisy, sloppy and a little wild. We were unkind to each other and fiercely loyal to each other, often on the same day. In short, we were an average family that just happened to have ten children.

Table of Contents

Brothers and Sisters: Why More When You Had Me?

Joe 3

Puss 5

Moe 6

Ginger 7

Gundi 8

Jonnie 9

Sandie 10

Mike 11

Pat 12

Chris 13

Parents, How to Raise Them

Promises 16

Warm Soup 18

The Smart Woman and the Genius 19

How the Cat Got the "M" on Its Forehead 20

Like Father, Like Daughter 21

The Power of Prayer, Really 22

Keeping the Faith 23

"A Rose By Any Other Name …" 25

A Valentine from Dad 27

Swimming and Life Lessons 29

Flowers, What's Not to Love? 30

The Apple Doesn't Fall Far from The Tree 31

The Best Present Ever 32

Letters from Home 33

The Will 34

You Can't Go Home Again 35

All in the Family

The Rescue..37

The Great Liver Scam...38

Educating Our Palates...39

Mom, Moe, Madame Alexander, and Me...........................40

Brothers, A Real Help When You Want to Learn Stuff 42

And Your Real Name Is?..43

Is This Yours? 45

Left and Lucky..47

The Joys of Moving to a New Place 48

Another Brother, Another Hero 50

Joe's Heart 51

How I Almost Saved a Mouse 52

Mom and Me...54

An Emergency Meeting of the Family.................................55

In Illo Tempus Conceptus Bonus Erat 57

My Inheritance 59

S & H Green Stamps, Popsicles, and Puss...........................61

Dad and Me...63

Memories of Sandie 64

The Middle Child

My First Confession and How I Learned All About Adultery 67

There's an "A" In Breast...68

Scull Nixes Head of High School Paper 70

"At Last, Exquisite Columbine, I Have Vanquished My Rivals ...".71

"In the Spring A Young Man's Fancy…" 72

Joan of Arc, St. Theresa, and Me 73

"It Ain't Me, Babe".. 74

No Woman Is an Island.. 75

Skiing, Sport or Torture?.. 76

The Expert and The Screw Up 78

The Best Comeback Ever... 79

"A Wind Is in The Heart of Me …".. 80

Husbands, They Can Be Trained

The Rules 82

A Funny Thing Happened …... 84

Out and About Inside Out 85

Tennyson's Brook and Paul 86

He Loves Me, He Loves Me Not 87

Basketball, Dads, and Legends 88

Gas and Diesel Fuel, How Different Can They Be? 89

There's Something About a Man with Scars 90

About Opposites Attracting ….. 91

Empty Nest.. 93

Children: Why When There Are Plants?

Jim.. 95

Gretchen.. 97

Stephanie... 99

Why Yes, I'll Chaperone... 100

The Role of Mary... 101

A Love Story... 103

The Stairs 105

A Funny Thing Happened on the Way to the Emergency Room ... 106

Teen Gretchen 108

Inchworm 109

Our Ethical Will..110

Caroline...111

Time Spent with Grandpa 112

Will's Heart..114

Out of the Mouths of Babes … 116

Pets, What Were We Thinking?

Killer 119

Samantha..121

Molly...123

Annie...124

Bridget and Me 125

In My Opinion

An Open Letter About Friendship, Our Daughters, and Abortion ..128

An Open Letter About Golf from Your Mother 130

"Alas for Those Who Never Sing…" 131

Costumes...133

Bet You a Nickel..135

My Sermon Would Be Better … 136

Ski Lesson 137

"The City"..139

Ecclesiastic Old Boys Club...140

The Ovation 141

Thank You 142

About the Author 143

Brothers and Sisters:

Why more when you had me?

Joe

First there was Joe. Ten years my senior, he was my hero. One day I came across him as he was painting our parents' bedroom walls. In the dwindling afternoon light, it was tough to tell whether the color he was painting was grey or blue.

So I asked him, "What color are you painting, Joe?"

With a perfectly straight face he said, "Yellow."

I inched further into the room, eyes huge with amazement. "Really? It looks blue to me."

"No," he continued. "It's a new kind of paint that goes on blue and dries a really pretty shade of yellow. If you come closer, you can see the place on this wall that's already beginning to change."

I worked my way across his splattered drop cloths and peered closely at the apparently blue soon-to-turn-yellow wall. And he painted my nose. I looked cross-eyed at the once freckled, now blue-gray feature and sighed. "It's not going to turn yellow, is it?" I asked.

"Nope," he said with a smile.

Another time, when I was eight years old, I saw Joe put a pretty gardenia corsage into an old, dented, tin bucket and then cover it with hay. Eyes popping, I asked him what the heck was he doing?

"I'm playing a joke on Judy," he whispered conspiratorially. "Want to help?"

Did I? Joe was my hero. Of course, I wanted to help. We picked eight or nine dandelions from our side yard and, with my excellent help, Joe fashioned a credible corsage. We used lacy white ribbon and some green leaves from our mom's prized hydrangea. Then we placed our handiwork on top of the hay that was on top of Judy's real corsage. I thought it looked pretty. I was eight.

"Are you going to give it to Judy now, Joe?" I asked in a hopeful voice.

"Yes," he answered absently as he turned the bucket this way and that. Then he looked more closely at me. "Do you want to walk down with me when I give it to her?"

So we went together: Joe, my brother, an eighteen-year-old high school senior, and me, his eight-year-old sister. We cut across the fields to bring Judy Regan, his prom date, a silly joke dandelion posy. It was one of the best days of my young life and he doesn't even remember it.

Puss

Mary Ellen is my oldest sister. Her nickname is Puss. We're not sure how she got that awful name, but that's what our family calls her.

She's five-foot-eight and a lefty. You can tell that she was an athlete by the way she moves. Her stride is long, her energy level always high. She never walked; she jogged. She never went up the stairs one at a time, and she was always whistling or singing, usually show tunes.

One of Puss's responsibilities as the oldest girl in the family was to encourage us to eat whatever awful, "healthy" food our mom had made us for dinner. We were a tough crowd, but she hit on a winning formula. It involved the song "Deep in the Heart of Texas." She would begin. "The stars at night, are big and bright..." Then she would clap four times and continue, "deep in the heart of Texas." When she clapped, we were supposed to bite, chew, and swallow a morsel of (for example) string beans. We did it so we could sing the next part of the song with her. It was a devious and brilliant plan. We all loved music and singing, especially with her. So it worked. I still salivate when someone applauds.

When Puss entered the Sisters of Mercy, she changed. I figured she was being tortured because she became calm and serene and holy acting. I wanted to help her escape but didn't know how. Then one Halloween she borrowed Joe and Moe's old army uniforms. She and another nun, dressed as military men, left the convent by the back door and went quietly around to the front. With stockings over their faces, they rang the bell. The elderly nun who answered the door was so intimidated by the "big boys" that she tried to give them all of the candy. The two "soldiers" politely declined. Each took one chocolate bar and left. After hearing that story, I figured Puss was okay, and that she was back to being normal.

Moe

Next came Moe. My mom once asked him to help me with my third-grade homework which was to memorize a famous poem. He said, "Sure," pleasantly, helpfully, which should have given her a clue. So we memorized the "Thirty Days Hath September" poem together.

Moe was merciless. "You have to get it right," he commanded. "You have to speak slowly and clearly," he counseled. In a little under an hour he said my delivery was perfect.

The next day at school, for the first time in my short life, I volunteered to recite the homework assignment. I stood up and slowly, confidently and clearly said:

"THIRTY DAYS HATH SEPTEMBER
APRIL; JUNE, AND NO WONDER
ALL THE REST EAT PEANUT BUTTER
EXCEPT FOR GRANDMA, SHE DRIVES A BUICK."

I got detention for three days, but it was worth it.

Moe also had the best secret boys' club, and I wanted to join it. "Sure," he said. "Just run as fast as you can and bang your head on the bathroom door." Which I did, and very well I might add. But Moe had such high standards, I had to do it twice before I got it right. Then he said, "Can't you read?" Actually, at that time the letters on the sign were a little fuzzy. "The sign says, BOYS ONLY." I was devastated. Not only did I not get into the club, it turned out that I was a girl, and if my headache was telling me anything, not a particularly bright one at that.

Ginger

Ginger is the fourth oldest in the family. Quietly generous, she would as quickly loan you her car as her lipstick. She is also the prettiest girl in our family. And although that's somewhat like being the best-looking aardvark in a zoo, still it's something.

Despite being a good student in school, Ginger would always "get" a joke two or three seconds after everybody else did. Naïve and trusting, she always fell for the tricks we played on her. She had, and still has, a sweetness and openness that should have shamed us pranksters, but of course it didn't.

One day I was being mean to Ginger. I'm not sure what it was all about, but I'm pretty sure there was some taunting going on. Incensed, she took her shoe off and threw it at me. I ducked, and the shoe broke the unusually shaped, hard-to-replace window behind me. My dad spanked Ginger for throwing the shoe and me for ducking.

Another summer day Ginger, Gundi, and I were playing in an old apple tree when our mom called us in for lunch. I swung down first and heard an ominous crack from our usual swing-down branch. I called a warning up to Gundi, but she was already standing next to me, shaking leaves from her T-shirt.

"Should we tell Ginger about the crack?" I asked.

"No," Gundi replied. "It held for me, so it will probably hold for…"

THUD! It was Ginger. She lay on her back, wheezing, gasping for breath, still clutching the errant branch in a desperate embrace.

"Go get Mom!" I yelled to Gundi. "I'll help Ginger!"

Gundi was bent from the waist, visibly shaking, dealing with what I thought were guilty tears. She gulped. "I can't! I'm laughing too hard."

Gundi

Gundi is the hardest of my siblings to compress into a thumbnail sketch. She is funny, smart, kind, and brave, and very, very dear to me. She has a thyroid condition which, combined with her husband's high blood pressure, precluded their having their own children. They adopted a special needs baby who is the light of their lives.

Gundi's real name is Gretchen, which is apt because of all of us, I believe she is the most like our mother, Gretchen, who was a terrific lady.

Gundi and I liked to call ourselves the collective middle child in our

family. She was the fifth child. I was the sixth. Our mom went on to have four more children, making the number of kids in the family ten. We used to drive our mom crazy, blaming our absurd, erratic behavior on our birth order. "Sorry Mom, it must be a 'Middle Child' thing…" we would chorus. We would look up Freudian words and phrases to toss into conversations at the dinner table, and our mom good-naturedly went along with this. Until, that is, we discovered the word *libido*.

Jonnie

I was born in the autumn. Perhaps that's why I have such an affinity with crisp October days and fire-warmed nights. Outgoing and gregarious, I never knew a stranger. There was always a common denominator to find and develop while I waited in line at the store, waited at the station for my train, or waited to get into the football game. As a consequence, I was everybody's pal but nobody's girlfriend. Eventually boys discovered me and I them, but I was and still am a small- town person with the inherent belief that the check is in the mail.

Sandie

Sandie was musically and academically gifted. She played the piano and four other instruments and was a member of Mensa. She was also a physical mess. She had more surgeries than I can count, had two miscarriages before she and Jack were blessed with their daughter Niki, and now has more metal in her body than a Ford Truck.

She wore thick glasses and had a hearing aid until one of her many surgeries took care of that particular problem. She was also a fruitcake who fortunately had a strong sense of humor and a wonderful daughter to help balance the uneven tenor of her adult life.

Sandie is the reason I have always felt that a beloved, happy childhood is the best gift a parent can give. Her large rowdy group of siblings and older parents were either the reason she kept on "keeping on" or the reason she had to.

Sandie was the first of us to die. Her time on earth was too short. There was so much more we wanted to share with her. All we can figure out about her death is that our mom, who passed away twenty years before Sandie, probably really did love her best and brought her home to be at peace.

Mike

Then there was Mike. While I was away at college, he'd found and shared my journal with his high school sweetheart. Apparently they garnered some comfort reading that Paul and I were going through the same soul searching with regard to "Hormones and the Church's Teachings." Later, I was glad he'd found an opportunity to discuss "dating" with me. I can remember thinking at the time *he's too young* and almost immediately realizing "No, no, he's not." Unprepared, I never got around to telling him that he shouldn't have let his girlfriend read my stuff. I was too caught up in the fact that our friendship as brother and sister was reaching a new and different level.

Mike is three years younger than I am and was always a bit small for his age. As his older and bigger sister, I had an obligation to pick on him. Arriving home from college one year, I remember calling out for him as I triumphantly sailed through the front door.

Mike's quiet "Here I am" was scarcely audible to me as I had my face caught in his T-shirt; my nose plastered to his belt buckle...

In the seven months I had been away at college, Mike had grown nearly a foot. I firmly believe one of the reasons Mike is such a "gentle giant" now is because he remembers what it was like to be the smallest kid. Now that he is six-foot-three and over two hundred pounds, I've let up on the bullying. I think he's had enough.

Pat

Pat says she was a Home Economics major in college because she couldn't make up her mind, but she's a natural when it comes to what used to be called the "womanly arts." A talented, creative needlewoman, she can as easily make a smocked-dress for her daughter as she can whip up two identical upholstered chairs for her twin grandsons. Her bread-baking day has total strangers baying at the moon outside her house, and her soups and cakes keep all of us more than willing to stop by.

A terrible driver, Pat has been known to close her eyes when things get a little tight, i.e. when parallel parking. One time, because she knew the way, she drove Moe, Puss, Gundi, and me to the movies. Parking spaces were at a premium, so we had to circle the building a few times. Pat drove up on the curb, an easy thing to do. As we came around again, she went up on the same curb. The third time around, as the front of the car rose still again, Moe said, "I think it's dead, Pat."

Chris

If ever there were a brother/sister look-alike contest, Chris and I would probably win. The youngest in the family and very bright anyway, Chris absorbed, like a cute freckled sponge, everything that went on around him. By the time he was seven, he had the vocabulary of a twelve-year old and the ability to be comfortable with people of all ages. My mother once told Chris if he disobeyed her it would be a sin.

Chris replied, "Don't be silly, Mother. I haven't reached the age of reason yet."

At that time the Catholic Church considered the age of seven to be the beginning of one's ability to reason – to know the difference between right and wrong – hence *the age of reason*. Chris not only understood this concept at the tender age of six. He'd also figured out how he could work it to his advantage.

The first time I ever stood up to my father was over his treatment of my brothers Mike and Chris, and I'm ashamed I waited as long as I did. I was twenty-two. My dad was a brilliant, driven man, but he was also an alcoholic. When he drank, he bullied the boys with words and actions. Mike was finally safely away in college, but Chris was the last soldier standing. Child number ten, he was being raised by parents the age of most of his friends' grandparents. And though I have great respect for our parents and all they did for us, they were worn out by the time Chris hit his teens.

My dad was super strict with him and when Chris rebelled sent him to a boarding school. This was a child weaned on our larger-than-life family, with its constant competition for food, attention, and the shower. Chris might have found some of that at a prep school, but not what he needed most: the knowledge that someone always had his back. When he ran away from the school, my dad called him a "horse's ass" and for a good while washed his hands of him. Chris finished his schooling with a PhD from Columbia.

When I asked him about my writing this, Chris said, "I think in some crazy way, Dad was trying to motivate me, and I guess it worked."

Parents, How to Raise Them

Promises

The woods are lovely, dark, and deep,
But I have promises to keep,
And miles to go before I sleep,
And miles to go before I sleep.
Robert Frost

My mother and I loved Robert Frost. Living in rural Connecticut, we recognized our land, our neighbors, and ourselves in his poetry. We had a grove of birch trees whose branches made great swings. We had a "good fences make good neighbors" neighbor. And "stopping by woods on a snowy evening" was something we both loved to do.

Maybe it was our shared sense of the absurd, but Mom and I often seemed to have the same response to our familial life. When I was fairly young, she explained symbolism to me. With that knowledge in hand, I understood why the words, "The woods are lovely, dark, and deep, but I have promises to keep" resonated so with her.

My mom had many "promises to keep." Whether they were meals to be prepared, laundry to be folded, or grappling children to separate, she always seemed to keep them.

Symbolically, I think her "lovely, dark, and deep woods" was her music. The concert grand piano in our living room was her steed, her solace, and for us, her children arriving home from school, a barometer of her every mood. Different composers' music signified different kinds of days. If, for example, Rachmaninoff was being played, it had been a tough one; if Bartok, there was a problem she was working on. Schubert or Brahms? There was probably a baby sleeping on the nearby couch. Beethoven? "God was in His heaven and all was right with the world."

Gershwin, specifically his *Rhapsody in Blue,* also signified that a good day had been had.

I don't play the piano, but I do have Alexa, a computerized musical device that plays whatever I ask for, whenever I ask. I can listen to my mother's favorite classics any time I choose, which is often. It's interesting: if Paul walks in the house and Rachmaninoff is playing, he turns around and goes back outside for a while.

I have no idea why.

Warm Soup

If my father were the type to "blow his own horn," which he was, he would have had a business card that read: Joseph Vincent Lane, Jr., Genius, Father, and *Chef Extraordinaire*, which he did.

The genius he probably was. He had advanced degrees from Fordham, Fordham Law, NYU, and Columbia. He used to tell us, "I got my first long pants when I graduated from Fordham."

Our response to this remark was usually a collective yawn.

I think his measure of success, as a father, probably began with the sheer number of his offspring. Then, the fact that all ten of us went to and graduated from schools of higher learning was added to his list of fatherly accomplishments.

The title of *Chef Extraordinaire,* which he had magnanimously bestowed upon himself, was another story. Dad made three meals which he called his *chef-d'oeuvres*.

The first was scrambled eggs with bacon. Neither the egg nor the bacon was ever fully cooked. And his secret ingredient was Worcestershire Sauce. His Sunday breakfasts were not a favorite with us.

The second prized recipe was Welsh rarebit, a British specialty, and Dad's favorite meal for meatless Friday suppers. Its ingredients were cheddar cheese, spices, mustard, Worcestershire Sauce, and beer – lots and lots of beer. Dad loved it. Our preference for frozen fish sticks on Fridays always puzzled him.

Dad's third, and, in his expert opinion, greatest performance in the kitchen was his "Day After Thanksgiving Turkey Soup." He would line up his sous chefs, his children, and have us pealing and chopping celery and carrots, chives and potatoes. Dad's job was to slice the turkey and add the spices. One year, he decided to enrich the recipe by adding wine. He had a generous hand with it. When it was nearly time for the soup to be soup, Dad sampled the broth. He sipped, grimaced, and sipped again. Then he addressed his hungry apprentices.

"Who wants fish sticks?"

The Smart Woman and the Genius

I've always known that my dad was a brilliant genius. I've known because he was always telling us, "Your father is a brilliant genius." If one of us performed especially well on a test or quiz, my dad would say, "Of course you did an excellent job. You've got my brains, haven't you?" My mom would smile and agree with him.

I can only remember my mom adding a comment once. She said something like, "And I suppose the children got their looks from my side of the family?"

My dad's head snapped up. I could tell he was reluctant to give up credit for anything, but he looked at the motley crew assembled for dinner and gave her permission to claim that part of us.

Time passed. We grew up. My sister Mary Ellen was going for her Masters' Degree in Child Psychology. As a part of her course work, she had to do a certain amount of testing, and what better test group than ten people living under the same roof? Among the many tests we took for her was an IQ test. And the results were amazing. My dad WAS a genius. BUT so was my mom. In fact, her IQ was higher than his.

I couldn't wait for her to tell him. I asked her, "When are you going to lower the boom, Mom?" and "Can I watch?"

My mother was furious! She yelled at Mary Ellen and she yelled at me. "I never gave your sister permission to tell the results of that test, and I forbid either one of you to let it go any further than this."

I was flabbergasted. Here she had the perfect means to stop my father's constant bragging and she wasn't going to use it?

Now that I've been married forty-five years, I can understand better what my mother was about. Anything that makes my husband unhappy or feel he is less of a person, makes me unhappy too. My mother really was a smart woman. I'm only now beginning to realize that there are a lot of smart women who have husbands who are geniuses.

How the Cat Got the "M" on Its Forehead

My mother and I were sitting on the floor of my brother's closet playing with Puff's kittens. They looked like fat, miniature tigers as they stalked our hands. While I stroked their tiny, furry bodies, my mom told me how the striped cat got the "M" on her forehead.

The Blessed Mother was having a terrible time getting the child Jesus to sleep. She sang him a lullaby; she rocked him in his cradle; and she carried him in her arms. But the baby was wide-awake.

The animals in the stable gathered around and watched Mary's efforts with interest. They respectfully asked her if they could help. Warmed by their kindness, Mary nodded.

The donkey reared (stood up on his hind legs), a trick he was secretly rather proud of. The child Jesus was delighted. He cooed and gurgled his baby approval.

The stable dog chased his tail round and round in a circle. This pleased the baby even more. He happily clapped his hands.

The ewes bleated several verses of their own special lamb lullaby, but the infant Jesus was more awake than ever.

A rather scruffy barn cat asked Mary if she could help, but the other animals laughed at her. "What makes you think you will succeed where we have failed?" they scornfully asked.

With a loving gesture, Mary silenced them and gave the cat her permission to try. First the cat perched at the foot of the cradle. She carefully licked each paw and groomed herself, smoothing her fur, combing her whiskers, patting her ears…the child Jesus was entranced. When the cat was as clean as could be, she gracefully jumped down onto the blanket that covered the little boy and proceeded to circle around and around looking for the perfect place to rest. Jesus' eyelids seemed to be getting heavy. Finally, the cat curled up into a ball and began to purr.

With a happy sigh the infant closed his eyes and slept.

To show her gratitude, Mary touched the cat on her forehead. Ever since that day, all striped cats have the letter 'M' on their foreheads.

I know this story is true because my mother told me.

Like Father, Like Daughter

At one of our family reunions, all ten of us "kids" got together for the first time in six years. My dad cleared his throat a few times and then proposed a toast to the family.

He looked around at the crowded table and spread his arms in a loving, albeit theatrical, gesture. "Look at this family," he said. "Which of these wonderful children could we have done without?"

Silence followed his words…for about a minute. Then Moe said, "Jonnie." Chris said, "Mike." Pat said, "Ginger." And on and on it went. We named every member of the family, all of our pets, and a few of the kids who lived with us until we realized we weren't related.

We all teased my dad. No matter how many of us gathered together, if one child, and I use the word loosely, was absent, he missed him.

Last week my daughter, Gretchen, went to Colorado to visit her best buddies there. At first, we all reveled in the silence. The phone refused to eat it missed her so much. Our daughter Steph spread her things all over the room they usually share, and her brother Jim became the only teen "in residence."

Then my husband Paul began to suffer. He had no one to "ground" for giving him "the look." No one argued with him over important matters like "makeup and fourteen-year-old girls," "skirts and their various uses," or "curfews and the twentieth-century teen."

Jim began yelling up the stairs at Gretchen for taking his CDs, U-2 vest, etc., only to realize she hadn't been home for three days. "Guess I'll have to blame Steph for taking my stuff till Gretch gets home again," he muttered.

Steph, the one who fights with Gretchen nonstop all day, every day, missed her immediately and was very vocal about it. "I miss Gretchen." she said. "It feels funny without her. When is she coming home?"

As for me, I didn't miss her at all. I didn't go into her room and think how empty it seemed. I didn't sit on her bed or play her awful tapes or read the funny sayings on her schoolbook covers. I didn't do these things because mothers are tough. I'm not like my dad at all.

The Power of Prayer, Really

My mother was a great believer in the power of prayer. She prayed for the repose of her parents' souls, she prayed for healthy babies, and she prayed for us, her children, all of the time. And she didn't restrict her prayers to spiritual matters. She was always happy to pray for good weather for the Notre Dame/Army game, for another win for the basketball team, or for the car to last just three more months. All of which met with my teenage approval.

But there came a time when our prayers, my mother's and mine, were for vastly different things. My mom wanted to give us to God. She felt there was no better path to eternal life than that of a nun or a priest. I would come home from a date or babysitting and go in to kiss her goodnight and there she would be: either still saying her prayers or asleep with the rosary beads cradled in her hands. This made me very nervous. I knew her most recent prayer project was…vocations.

What worried me about that? I'll tell you. Never one to settle for small numbers, my mom prayed for three of her children to hear the call to give their lives to God. Heck, with one vocation out of ten, I stood a pretty good chance of getting by, but three out of ten? I knew I was a goner.

Then one of the good nuns at school told me that the prayers of a sinner or a child are always answered. I knew I fit into both of those categories, so I began a prayer campaign that would have put the pope to shame.

My mother would pray in her room and I would pray in mine, hoping my prayers were canceling hers, like a stamp. I told God, as nicely as possible you understand, that I did not want a religious vocation, thank you.

My sisters Mary Ellen and Sandie entered the Sisters of Mercy. My sister Gretchen entered the Sisters of the Divine Compassion. I was happy for them and happy for me, because by then I had met Paul and was praying for good weather for his college baseball games. And that he'd have the good sense to marry a nice sinner like me.

Keeping the Faith

Both of my parents were practicing Catholics, with my mom practicing more than my dad. Actually, in matters of faith, I'm more like my father. We were both what is called "cafeteria Catholics." This meant we would pick and choose which tenets of our faith to believe and follow.

Born with a congenital hip problem, my dad would sit and drink his scotch while the rest of us, in the months of May and October, knelt to say the Rosary. He would intone the first half of the Hail Mary in the most solemn of voices but spoil the effect by sipping his drink when one of us said our part.

The Rosary is broken up into five segments of beads. For each bead in a decade, or set of ten, there is a Hail Mary to be prayed. Since we <u>had</u> to say the Rosary, we kids got to be competitive as to who got to say the most prayers, and who could say them the fastest.

If all ten of us were home; we would each get only five Hail Marys to say. If a guest were visiting, getting one of our segments to pray would honor that person but irritate us kids.

One time Moe came in from a spring night's baseball game with a friend in tow.

With an imperious gesture, Dad motioned to the teen to kneel and join us. He protested.

"But, Mr. Lane, I'm Jewish."

"All the more reason to teach my children another way to pray," Dad rejoined.

So Ham Styron knelt with us and we taught him the Hail Mary.

My dad studied the writings of the apostle Paul in the original Greek. He loved all of Paul's epistles but most especially his second letter to Timothy in which Paul wrote of his impending death: "Even now I am being poured out like a libation. The hour of my dissolution is near. I (have) fought the good fight. I (have) finished the race. I (have) kept the faith."

This became my dad's mantra.

- **Fight the Good Fight,** he would state. Don't waste your time and efforts on things that won't matter down the road.
- **Finish the Race.** He didn't say we had to win the race. He said we had to finish what we started, even if we knew we weren't going to win or succeed. This was really hard to do.
- **Keep the Faith.** If we were going out on a date, or with friends, my father would call out from the corner of the living room. "Don't forget to keep the faith."

As you can image, that was a real show stopper.

Although a good man, my dad was an alcoholic. Brilliant, clever, and demanding when sober, he was mean and caustic when drinking. His standards for us, his children, were high. He hoped we would follow his "do as I say, not as I do" ethos.

As an adult I can better see what he was trying to teach us. The devil he was fighting was alcohol. He tried to fight the good fight. He tried to finish the race. He tried to keep the faith.

He tried.

"A Rose By Any Other Name ..."

When I was nine, I heard my mother bemoaning my brother's name.

"What's wrong with Moe's name?" I asked her.

She replied. "His real, legal, and baptismal, name is Paul Allen."

My face must have been a study. Incredulous, I asked her, "Really? Wow!"

I knew my oldest brother, Joe, was named for my father.

I also knew my oldest sister, Mary Ellen, was named for my paternal grandmother.

"So," I asked, "who was Moe, I mean, Paul Allen, named for?"

My mom said, "An ancestor whose roots trace our family back to the Mayflower."

"Oh," I said. "Okay. Can I have an orange?"

My grandmother lived in our home for twenty years. She took over two rooms on the second floor and had them made into an apartment. She was imperious and stuffy and not very nice to my mother. We shared meals with her when she deigned to honor us with her presence.

There were always things we children did that gave her reason to correct both us and our mother, as obviously, mom was not teaching us proper etiquette.

Because of her behavior, I always thought *she* was the one descended from the Pilgrims. She was snooty enough and old enough, in my opinion, to actually *be* a Pilgrim. Imagine my surprise when I discovered, and read, the book about our genealogy that had been tucked away in the attic.

My mother was the heir apparent! It was *her* ancestors who had come over on the Mayflower.

I had trouble getting my head around my grandmother's arrogance. So I asked my mom. "Why? Why is she so mean?"

My mom explained. "She is unhappy because she has to live with us. She would rather have her own house but can't afford one. Be kind to her, Jonnie. If you can't be kind, be respectful. She is your grandmother and you owe her that."

Class, real class,
is best taught by example.
My mom was a master teacher.

A Valentine from Dad

In my family, it was always my mom who wrote the cards and letters. Whether we were at camp or college or just in the uncertain young married phase of our lives, she was able to let us know in "a hundred words or less" that we were loved and understood.

In the autumn of my freshman year in college, Kevin, my high school boyfriend, who was also a freshman in college, invited me to his school's Centennial Ball. My freshman year was my sister Gretchen's junior year in college and my sister Sandie's junior year in high school and my brother Mike's sophomore year there, etc. etc. I believe you can get a picture of my family's educational/financial status and the place Kevin's invitation held in my parents' scheme of things.

I got a job. Already on a service scholarship, which meant I was a general dogs-body for my school; I waited and bussed tables in the dining room and checked out and stacked books in the library. No big deal. So, on weekend nights, I took phone orders for room service at the White Plains Hotel. Kevin was in Philadelphia, and I was in love, so this seemed like a good idea at the time.

My wages went into a "Centennial Ball" stash. I would need train fare, a dress and shoes, and something sophisticated and collegiate to wear coming and going. As January approached, Kevin's letters came less and less frequently, but we were both in the throes of exams, so I wasn't worried.

Two weeks to go, I gave in and called him. "Where was I staying? When would he be able to meet me? How did his finals go?"

Kevin seemed surprised. Did I still think we were going out together? He had asked someone else he'd been seeing…I made some inane comment about how we would make the *next* Centennial Ball and hung up. The damn call cost me eight dollars.

My mom was great. Supportive and warm, she figuratively held my hand over a long phone call. This time, I reversed the charges.

But it was a note from my dad that made everything right. He'd taken one of my youngest brother Chris's Valentine cards and finished the silly verse. It read:

    "Valentine be mine." My dad had added.

    "And not some dope's who's got no spine.

    "You are too grand, you wonderful gal,

    "To mope over babies from LaSalle."

Fifty years later, in Pilgrim Hall Museum, I was intrigued by a collection of letters written by a Civil War boy-soldier to his mother. They could have been mine. Inane, unsubstantial, and somewhat whiney, they complained about the food, the inadequate accommodations, and the clothing that gave little warmth…He was not asking his mother for money or clothes. He was asking her if she loved him and missed him.

Her letters of response were not featured in the display, but I like to think she did love him and miss him. I like to think his dad did too.

Swimming and Life Lessons

My dad promised each of the ten of us that he would toss us off the dock into the Long Island Sound if we hadn't learned to swim by the time we turned six. We knew it would happen, but happily ignored the fact until our fifth birthdays. Then we would actually try to learn to swim.

In the back of my mind, I knew my mom wouldn't let me drown. But also in the back of my mind, I knew my dad would make good his promise. So, I began to teach myself how to swim.

Step One: The Doggie Paddle – If our dogs, who chased their tails all the time actually thinking someday they would catch them, could do the doggie paddle, so could I.

Step Two: Water Depth – The water below the dock of my dad's choice was pretty shallow. I could pretend to be swimming while actually standing up.

Step Three: Fooling Dad – See Steps One and Two.

As my sixth birthday approached (October 21) I wondered if I would get a reprieve because of my autumnal beginnings…not so, my brother Moe assured me. His birthday is November the sixth and he said he hit the water wearing a sweater and blue jeans.

I was doomed.

All summer long I worked on my crawl. That's what my mom called it: "The Crawl." With inner tube, without inner tube, the results were the same. I sank like a moss-covered rock. I knew I was going to be the "one less mouth to feed" my mom was always talking about.

Then things changed. I met a girl named Lillian. She was afraid of the water. She didn't know how to swim, and she was already six! So I said I would teach her how to swim.

"But first," I asked, "when is your birthday?"

Flowers, What's Not to Love?

Flowers? My father loved them. Actually, he loved to look at them. We, his lucky children, got to plant them, fertilize them, de-bug them, deadhead them, and seasonally replace them with other flowers that needed to be planted, fertilized, de-bugged, and deadheaded.

One spring, Dad decided we needed a rose arbor. He ordered forty plants from Jackson and Perkins and had us pace off two parallel rows that would soon be glowing with his flowers, whose colors would melt from red to pink to white to yellow.

After we dug the trenches and put rose dust in the furrows, we planted his babies. Days blended into weeks and there were no buds, no flowers. What we did have was hundreds of Japanese Beetles. Ever the arbitrator, Dad made a contract with us. For every Japanese Beatle we caught, we would get a nickel.

We enthusiastically began to herd those tiny 'doggies' into flour sacks. Chris even went to our neighbor's yards to bag some of theirs.

We each made a fortune, sometimes as much as $4. And, I firmly believe, Japanese Beatle moms started telling their little larvae to avoid our property.

Back to Dad's rose grotto, we suspected our beautiful experiment had been planted too close to our six acres of apple trees. Deer, coming in at night for a dessert of Macintosh windfalls, soon found they preferred the gourmet fare of rose petals and, later, rosehips.

Fifty years later, I still have an antipathy towards this special bloom. My husband, Paul, now has American Beauties in his garden. He tends them as though they are his babies, with special rose food and talks about the dangers of beetles…

When he's not looking, I kick them.

The Apple Doesn't Fall Far from The Tree

"Mom says we have to gather a couple of bushels of *windfalls* for Mrs. Kitchen's pigs," called Ginger. She cupped her hands to make a megaphone even though we were only two feet above her and continued. "And she said now would be a good time."

In our cellar there were enough paper-wrapped apples to last our family the entire winter. There would be pies and crumbles and fritters and applesauce for months to come. Since we were all set, our Mom was now making us share the ones that had fallen, or been blown down, hence the term *windfalls*, with our neighbor's farm animals.

Sandie, Mike, Pat, and I had been sitting cross-legged in an apple tree on our Ping-Pong table fort planning our next rotten apple battle. Mike groaned. "Last time, Mom gave all the good ones to the Kitchens. It was just not right."

Like the monkeys we were, we swung down onto the ground and, with ill grace, began to pile up our pulpy over-ripe apple weapons. Sandie got some bushel baskets and we filled three of them to overflowing.

Pat groused. "Who says the apple doesn't fall far from the tree? These are all over the place."

Ginger opened her mouth to explain the cliche, looked at her surly siblings, and closed it again.

Bantering back and forth, we walked the half-mile to Mrs. Kitchen's. When she saw us and our bounty, her eyes filled with tears.

"You are such wonderful children," she said. "I pray for your beautiful family all the time."

On the walk home, Pat said, "Maybe we could pick up a few more."

Three bushels later, we were back up in our Ping-Pong table fort. Leaning back on his elbows, Mike said, "I'm glad I had the idea to help Mrs. Kitchen."

The Best Present Ever

I was six years old when I noticed my mother was pregnant (with Chris, my soon-to-be youngest brother). My seventh birthday was coming up and I wondered if things were going to work out for me.

Totally unselfishly, I would ask her ten, sometimes twelve, times a week, "Am I going to have a birthday party this year, Mom?" She was due to give birth ten days before my birthday. Plenty of time, in my six-year old's estimation, to recover from giving birth for the eleventh time. Plenty of time to set up and run a fabulous seventh birthday party for me, her really nice daughter.

I didn't have a party that year. To make up for it, my mom told me I could have Chris, that he was my gift; that he would always be my special little brother.

I liked that, a lot. Still do. Chris, not so much.

Not long after Mom gave Chris to me, Mrs. Fagan came to visit. She said something like, "I can't wait to see that darling boy."

So I said, "I'll get him," and ran upstairs. I got Chris out of his crib, carefully holding his head, as it still wobbled a bit. Then I had a great idea! Instead of carrying him all the way downstairs – twelve steps down, then, at a right angle, four more to the landing, then four more to the first floor, I'd just hold him over the banister, so she could see him.

Mrs. Fagan shouted something in a language that I didn't know. My mom calmly said, "Joan Mary, just bring your brother down using the stairs please." I should have gotten the clue that she, too, was somewhat rattled because she used *Joan Mary*, my important name.

Somehow Chris survived his possessive, adoring sister and her lessons.

I taught him how to spit, how to ride a trike, and later, a bike, how to spit better, so the spit would make it further out of his mouth and not dribble down his t-shirt, and how to hang upside down from a tree branch for a long time and not throw up.

When Chris started school, he excelled. I'm pretty sure it was because I had already taught him all the important stuff.

Letters from Home

I've been sitting at the kitchen island, warming my psyche with a cup of tea and an old letter from my mom. She wrote it to me my senior year at college. There were four of us in college that year, and things were "tough all over."

My twentieth birthday had come and gone, and the usual bizarre birthday package that only my mother could devise had not arrived. There was only a letter in my box.

"Dear Joan Mary," it began. I panicked. I'm only called Joan Mary on state occasions or in emergencies. I quickly scanned the rest of the letter. It went on to explain there would be no gift this year, that the four tuitions were proving to be a heavy burden. But, my mom continued, she could send her love, her belief in the beautiful young woman I had become, and her prayers for me on this very special occasion.

I can still remember my disappointed, immature reaction. I sat in a corner of the lounge with tears of self-pity trickling down my face. One of my suitemates saw me and asked what was wrong. Wordlessly, I handed her the letter. She read it through, then read it again. She swallowed loudly and then stunned me with her reaction.

Mary Ellen, who had everything my greedy little heart desired – clothing, coins in her jeans, her own car – envied me! I listened open-mouthed to her catalogue of the wonderful things I possessed: my family, our closeness, our shared sense of humor, and, especially a mother who would write a beautiful letter like that.

With my tail between my legs, I crept off to write a thank you letter to my parents. I'm embarrassed to say it was the first letter of thanks I had written in a very long time.

My mom used to say that when her psyche needed a lift, she would reread my letter.

Things come full circle, don't they?

The Will

After my dad's funeral, my brother Mike, his executor, asked the nine of us to come together to discuss "things." With a pitch like that, who could resist?

My father, an attorney, had been known for his ability to spend creatively. None of us had expectations of a windfall. Actually, none of us had expectations at all. Feeding, clothing, and educating the ten of us had been a major undertaking, one our parents had taken on with style, grace, and humor. Little was left at the completion of this but educated offspring who had a lot to say and furnishings that had been through the mill, literally and figuratively.

Oh, my parents had once had beautiful things; we just destroyed them. My brother Chris added a cave to an oil painting my father particularly cherished. It had been taken down from the wall for spring cleaning and left in a tempting, easy-to-reach location for a five- year old with a curtain rod sword. That was pretty much the story of all of our parents *lares and penates*. The child and the article of furniture might differ, but the results would be the same.

Be that as it may, apparently my father had made two wills. The first divided his estate into ten equal parts. The second earmarked three of my siblings and gave them a larger inheritance than the seven remaining. Mike, ever honest, felt we should be made aware of both. My father, a brilliant attorney, was also a parent. Since the second will was never signed, the state of Ohio did not acknowledge its existence. Apparently, my father had sent the second document to his lawyer with expressed misgivings and no signature...Now Mike was asking us to express our opinions one way or another.

"You can't go back home to your family.
Back home to your childhood …
You can't go home again."
Thomas Wolfe

You Can't Go Home Again

After Paul and I got engaged, my mom had me come into the den for a little *talk*. I smiled, thinking it would be along the lines of the proverbial birds and bees parent-child talk, but my mom seldom did the expected.

"Jonnie," she began. "Paul is a good man. You are a fairly good woman." We grinned at each other. "I expect you to make your marriage work, because Thomas Wolfe was right. *You can't go home again*. Home is now a place to visit, not to stay."

Since I had similar thoughts along these lines, I happily accepted her familial wisdom.

My sister Sandie got engaged a year after I did. I happened to be visiting home when she came out of the den after her *talk* with Mom. She was a little weepy, so I put my arm around her shoulders.

"So, had your mom talk, did you?" I asked, giving her a sideways hug.

"Yes," she replied. "But it really got me when Mom said, 'This is your home and there will always be a place here for you.'"

Years later, I came to see that my mom knew her chicks, as Sandie did go home to stay a few times. I'm still not sure if my *mom talk*, with the Thomas Wolfe reference, was a compliment. Being me, I'm inclined to believe it was.

All in the Family

The Rescue

Three young children were sitting on a log in what were obviously their usual places. Two younger siblings played in the piney sand nearby. The morning sun's rays haloed mop tops of ginger, strawberry blonde, and auburn. With the ease of a routine long established, they chatted and waited for their salty wet bathing suits and skin to dry.

Suddenly one of them pointed skyward and said, "Look!"

An Osprey flew into their private Eden and onto their dock with balletic grace. Long slender wings of grey, gilded with gold, slowly fanned the air as the majestic bird landed.

In awe-filled silence the children gaped. They scarcely breathed for fear of frightening their beautiful trespasser.

As for the Osprey, it seemed to be posing for their edification. It turned its head slowly, first to the left, then to the right, then spread its wings, like a model showing the lines of a designer mink coat. Finally, it settled on the faded grey railing of the dock as if it were planning to stay for a while.

Suddenly, abruptly, one of the children ran at the bird. Shouting and flapping her arms, she yelled, "Go away! Scram! Beat it!"

Now gawky in its efforts to get away, the frightened bird cawed raucously and flapped up and away.

"Why'd you do that, Patty?" her sisters and brothers angrily queried as their sister turned with a happy grin.

She smiled. "I just saved its life."

Snorts of disbelief followed that remark.

"No," she said, serious now.

"Last night I heard Mom and Dad talking. Mom said, 'Five children is enough. If I ever see that damn stork again, I'm going to shoot it.'"

The Great Liver Scam

The only members of my family who liked liver were our two collies, our cats, and my parents. The rest of us – now in our fifties, sixties, and seventies – still shudder whenever it is mentioned.

Wednesday was always liver night. There could be great famine, floods, and plagues. War could be declared. Our house could burn down, and my mother would still find some way to give us liver. She was determined to prepare meals that were *nutritional* as well as filling. My father was equally determined that we develop educated palates. So we suffered...until I was eleven when my older brothers and sisters developed the liver scam.

One of the big kids would take a small bread plate and pass it beneath the table to another. Slowly, each child moved his liver from his dinner plate to the bread plate which made its way the length and breadth of the table right under our parents' noses until it returned to its source, heavily laden with nutritious, palate-enriching liver.

We kids began to look forward to Wednesday nights, wondering how Moe or Gretchen would dispose of the evidence this time. (Our collies, King and Snuffy, had beautiful coats that winter.) Mother was triumphant as she looked around the table at our bright faces, reassured that we'd come to appreciate at least one of the finer things in life.

When I went to college and learned more about the cost of things, I developed guilty feelings about all of the expensive meat we'd been feeding the dogs over the years. I wanted to tell my parents, but Sandie, Mike, Pat, and Chris were still at home. Could I turn traitor? Could I 'narc' on my siblings?

Thomas Paine once wrote, "He who would safeguard his own freedom, would secure even his enemy from oppression." I interpreted this to mean that if I wanted a liver-free future for myself, I'd have to keep up my brothers' and sisters' cover.

We never told my parents. When we went out to dinner with them, no one ever "felt in the mood" for liver. And under no circumstances would any of us ever visit them on a Wednesday.

Educating Our Palates

Saturday nights and Sunday's dinners were always about "educating our palates."

Our dad would set up the menu, and our mom would prepare the gourmet fare.

For the most part, we children didn't know what palates were, and didn't care if ours were stupid or uneducated. But our dad would insist. There would be shrimp or scallops as appetizers, along with what we called "stinky cheese" – Liedekranz – on toast, as pre-dinner fare.

Potatoes, which we loved, would be ruined, because our mom would mix scallions or cheese into them. Other vegetables we loved were not invited to the feast. This meant no corn or carrots or string beans. However there would be beets or Brussels sprouts or asparagus, each of which would lie in naked splendor on our plates. Sometimes there would be hollandaise sauce or gravy, but try though they might, they couldn't deaden the taste of the awful things beneath them.

As for the entre, swordfish, steak, and lamb were the go-to specials, with clams and other shellfish filling in during the summer. My brothers made me cry when they told me the lamb was the "little lamb that Mary had."

Another time, when Mom served us cow's tongue, Moe had us all in stitches by pretending to be a tongue-less cow trying to moo. He said "ooth," acting like a lisping cow, four or five times. Pat laughed so hard her milk came out her nose.

Our poor mother, after hours of preparing amazing meals, would look at the uninspired faces of her assembled offspring and sigh.

"Joe," she'd begin, "maybe we could bring teaching the children about the finer things in life down to just once a week." Our dad in somewhat of a snit would reluctantly agree.

But our punishment on nights like that would be "No dinner. No dessert."

Mom, Moe, Madame Alexander, and Me

The Christmas when I was twelve was a very special one for me. I was the tomboy of the neighborhood. I could climb a tree faster than anybody. I could stand on my bicycle seat and ride down the street, and I could hit a baseball as far as my brothers could. All of which were very important to me.

But when my mother asked me what I wanted for Christmas, I looked carefully around to be sure no one heard me and asked her for a doll.

"Are you sure, Jonnie?" she asked.

I can still see her sitting at the piano, giving me one of those quizzical mother-type looks. When I nodded my asset, still afraid one of the other kids might hear or see us, she let the subject drop.

In the weeks that followed, I was sorely tempted to tell my mom I had changed my mind. Especially nerve racking was the thought of what the other kids would say when I opened up a doll. I looked for a chance to get her alone, but the "small fry," my younger brothers and sisters, were being especially good and they wanted to be sure Mom saw all their goodness so she could tell Santa, so she was never alone.

By the time Christmas arrived, I was a wreck. I wondered if a dumb doll was worth all the anxiety I had gone through. Then I opened the box. A Madam Alexander Doll was inside, and she was beautiful. My mom had made my doll several extra outfits, and I couldn't wait to try them on her. I was rummaging in the box, sifting through the sweaters and skirts when Moe caught sight of me.

He did an exaggerated doubletake and stage whispered, "Well would'ya get a load of that? Jonnie got a doll!"

Everybody looked at me. I could feel my face getting red, but I couldn't think of anything to say. My mom took over.

She said, "I gave your sister a doll because I felt it was time she tried some feminine pursuits. Have you a problem with that?"

Of course, no one did. Only a fool would cross his mother on Christmas Day. She might take something back.

I'd love to tell you I still have that doll and that I gave her to my daughter Gretchen when she was twelve, but we used my doll as bait to get a huge snapping turtle to move forward. He clamped his beaky mouth on her head and smashed her eyes in. Too bad. She was a great doll.

Brothers, A Real Help When You Want to Learn Stuff

I've always loved sports. Even when I was fairly young, doing well athletically was important to me. But then any girl with four brothers has to learn to be agile. Simply staying out of their way requires consummate skill. In his own way, each of my brothers helped me become the outstanding athlete I am today.

Moe used to chase me. When he'd catch me, I'd have to kiss the floor and say, "I love you, floor." Since this was not much fun, I got to be a pretty good long-distance runner.

Joe was much nicer. He helped me with my hand-eye coordination. His place was next to mine at the dinner table. I would ask my mom for seconds in meat and potatoes and pass my plate via Joe to her. My plate would always come back loaded with vegetables. Joe's plate, on the other hand, was always full of meat and potatoes. For years I thought my mom had a hearing problem.

Then there was the summer Mike and Chris taught me how to play basketball. Although they were pretty thin at the time, two six-foot-three-inch tall guys, thin or not, can do a lot of damage to a five-foot five-inch girl, especially a sister. Having seen them play with their girlfriends, I figured they would treat me with the same gentle solicitude should one of them bump, trip, or tread on me. I was wrong.

Although they were pretty rough, my brothers never meant to hurt me. The time they broke my nose, they felt terrible. But I forgave them everything. I adored them. Even now, the only grudge I bear them is the fact that I had to eat a caterpillar to join their secret club and my sister Gundi got in by making brownies. But, then, she's not as good an athlete as I am.

And Your Real Name Is?

Everyone in my family has a nickname. Mine has always been Jonnie. My real name is Joan Mary, but no one ever called me that except the teachers at St. Mary's Grammar school. And even they soon gave up because I never answered to it. I'd sit at my desk and wonder who the fresh girl was who wouldn't answer Sister Anita.

My brother Mike had a similar problem. I came first, you see, and my nickname was *Jonnie.* When he came along with the legitimate name of John Michael, "Jon" had already been taken. So, he was always *Mike.* He never answered to his proper name either. The good nuns had us both take hearing tests and they were baffled by our scores. It took my mom and some interesting stories to get us out of that one.

For a while after that silly mix up, my mother insisted on calling us by our given names. That didn't work out very well either, because she normally only called us by our proper names when we had misbehaved. She'd call me to fold some wash, and I'd peer anxiously around the corner.

"Are you mad at me, Mom?"

"No, Dear," she'd answer. "I just need a hand with the laundry."

"Well, you didn't have to call me 'Joan Mary.' I would have come if you called me by my real name."

My mother sighed.

When Paul and I had our first girl baby, we chose the name 'Gretchen' in honor of my mother. We called her from the hospital to tell her the good news.

"Well, that's lovely dear," said my mother, "but Gretchen isn't my real name. Didn't I ever tell you that story? Your Uncle Hans and I tried to run away when he was five and I was three. We got as far as the corner and had to turn back because neither of us was allowed to cross the street. All of my brothers and sisters called me Gretchen from then on. You know, Hans and Gretchen? My real name is Elizabeth

Regina." There was a long silence at my end. I wonder if my mother ever learned that Hansel's sister was named Gretel, not Gretchen.

Nicknames, whether nice or mean, are a part of the fabric of our lives. I guess the bottom line is the way the name is said. Even a name like "Stinky" said with affection can be music to the ears. Even a name like "Jonnie."

Is This Yours?

As stated in the introduction, our living room was fifty-four feet by forty feet. It was majestic, imposing, and somewhat daunting to newcomers. The interior walls were stone. The floors were marbleized concrete. Our beloved home had been built to be a Cadillac showroom. Its location, four miles from the town of Norwalk, Connecticut, was Cadillac's bad luck and our good fortune.

My dad bought it and settled us in. And, although we were ten in number, we children were hard put to do any lasting damage to the place. The fortress' strengths aside, my dad had strict rules about his "summer palace." We were not allowed to eat anything anywhere near its most recent acquisition, the TV.

One section of the living room held our fourteen-foot-long dining table with its requisite benches and chairs. This is where we had most of our meals. Thus, in my dad's opinion, there was no excuse for a person to eat any type of food near his latest toy.

One Saturday afternoon, Dad found orange peels on the table next to his prized TV.

He gathered us, *the small fry*, the five youngest children, and began his cross-examination. Ever the attorney, he paced back and forth, hands clasped behind his back, solemnly intoning the awful, possibly legal ramifications for our behavior.

No one would admit to the wrongdoing. Dad thought we were being loyal to each other and got tougher. He left the kitchen and returned with a Ping-Pong paddle. One of us snorted; it could have been me. He looked so silly brandishing his absurd sword of retribution. He couldn't get an admission of guilt from any of us, so he lined us up with our backs to him and whacked each one of us with the paddle.

It didn't hurt. But I was annoyed that whoever did the deed hadn't owned up. Dad left the room, and we all looked at each other with the special loathing only siblings can generate. The silence was heavy, with only the aggrieved rubbing of our posteriors to indicate what had just happened.

Our dad came back into the kitchen, thinking that, by now, we would have ferreted out who the guilty party was. While we were all glaring at each other, and at Dad, our older sister, Ginger, came home. Not in the least sensitive to the hostile atmosphere, she kissed our dad, looked around the room and said, "Oh good, you picked up my orange peels. I forgot all about them. Thanks."

Our dad looked at her, then at us, then at the Ping-Pong paddle, then at the peels.

He said, "I think you five can work out how your sister should be punished." Then he left the room.

Left and Lucky

We were on our way to visit my sister Mary Ellen, who was in the convent in Madison, Connecticut. Together, Uncle Hans and my family were going to visit the Sisters of Mercy's Novitiate there.

Uncle Hans suggested we stop for ice cream on the way, and five of my brothers and sisters, two cousins, and I, thought it was a great idea.

We clambered out of the two stuffed station wagons and lined up in a Dairy Queen parking lot.

With my vanilla, always vanilla, ice cream cone in hand, I strolled around the side of the building. There I met and fell in love with an old dog with a white muzzle and a timidly wagging tail. I sat down next to him and we shared my two scoops. When we had licked the cone clean, I went back around the corner toward our car.

It was gone. They both were. My dad was driving one car, my Uncle Hans the other. Each thought the other had me in a vehicle crammed full of kids.

The proprietor of the Mom and Pop Dairy Queen was more upset than I was. He kept giving me pats on the head and free ice cream, saying, "I'm sure your family will be back soon, Sweetheart."

I, basking in all the attention, went back to my doggy pal and we played the afternoon away.

When my family finally returned, I pretended to be miffed. But, secretly, I knew, I had had a better day than my brothers and sisters and cousins had.

They had to hang out with nuns for hours, being "polite and well-mannered." I had the dog and ice cream and head pats.

Even as a ten year old I knew who was lucky, and, it wasn't the kids at the convent.

The Joys of Moving to a New Place

We all laughed at my dad when he said we were moving to Ohio. He had to be joking. People who live twenty years in one place don't just up and move. Besides, my dad used to think he was really truckin' if he walked from the living room to the kitchen. Didn't he realize what an effort it would be to move us all?

As I began to believe him, I could see there might be some compensation for leaving my beloved home town. Norwalk was a nice place, but everybody knew us. This was my mother's fault. All ten of us look like carbon copies of each other. If I were to try to sneak a cigarette, someone would surely take it out of my mouth and say something like, "You're one of the Lanes, aren't you? Your mother is such a lovely person. I'm sure she wouldn't want her daughter to smoke..."

My dad and brothers wouldn't let any of us girls go to the drive-in movies either. One time I went with my latest beau, secure in the knowledge that both of my older brothers were away at school. It didn't matter. One of the guys who sold tickets at the gate yelled at me and told the others selling tickets the same old story. "She's Joe's sister, and she's not allowed in."

Yes, Ohio was looking better and better.

Our first few days in our new state held many a learning experience for the kids from Connecticut. One of the first new rules we came up against was the Upper Arlington leash law. Mike, my clever brother, made a huge long leash that kept the police, the neighbors and our country-bred dogs happy. The first few days Mike walked the dogs. He then decided to share the honor. I didn't mind. There were some cute guys in our neighborhood. I dressed up in my newest t-shirt and shorts and wore my sandals with the three-inch heels. The dogs weren't impressed at all. They ran me for four blocks, pulled a quick U-turn and headed for home at a dead run. I was keeping up pretty well, although

48

they were around a corner hedge before I was. I heard the commotion before I added to it by falling at the feet of our next-door neighbor. I apologized as I tried to disentangle the dogs and their leashes from his wheelbarrow, which had been full of cow manure. But he wouldn't hear a word of it.

He laughed and said, "You're one of the Lanes, aren't you?"

49

Another Brother, Another Hero

When I was a senior in college, my brother Moe came to see me. He stayed for a few hours and we caught up on family news.

Six years older than me, and brilliant, he received a four-year scholarship to Fairfield Prep, a Jesuit high school in CT. There he won academic awards, a poetry prize, and was the star catcher for the varsity baseball team. When he graduated from The Prep, he got another four-year academic scholarship, this time to Boston College, where he also played baseball. A gifted athlete, he was also scouted by the then New York Giants

Moe messed around, didn't study, and drank himself out of BC and straight into alcoholism. That he came to visit me was amazing. I hadn't seen him in a year. I knew he was working in Connecticut but did not know where or for whom.

A college senior, I was pretty much on my own financially. I had a work-service scholarship, took orders for room service at the White Plains Hotel, ironed my friends' clothing, for a price, and received $15 every two weeks from my dad.

Near the end of his visit, Moe asked me if I could loan him some money. When I explained my three-job work schedule, he visibly blanched. He then reached into his wallet, gave me a ten-dollar bill, and left.

Moe has been chemically clean for more than forty years. He went back to school, got his degree, and now works with addicts like himself. He is another one of my brothers who is my hero.

Joe's Heart

I sat down heavily on the park bench, and boldly began…

"Pat called. She was crying. That didn't bother me much because as a family we are criers. We cry at refrigerator commercials, we weep over roadkill, and don't even get me started on that scene in *Bambi* where Bambi and his father, the young and the old stag, are standing together on a ridge and the old stag turns and walks away. It gets me every time. Our dad used to say that our bladders were next to our eyes. So I just, casually, asked her, 'What's up?'

"'It's Joe,' she said.

"I sat up taller. 'What about Joe?'

"Joe is our oldest brother. He went back to school at age sixty-four to get his Masters at NYU. He rollerblades all over Manhattan looking like Ichabod Crane without the horse. And his door is always open to us, his younger siblings. He is our hero, our damn bulletproof hero.

"'He's having heart surgery, a triple bypass,' she told me.

"I swore.

"'When? Where? How? How did you find out? I just spoke with him on the phone, the jerk!'

"Pat said, 'He said he didn't want us to worry.'

"Our family, a large one, has a calling list for emergencies, birth and wedding announcements, and weather anomalies. I'm not Pat's person to call, so I knew she was scared. We called Nora, Joe's wife, to get her input, discussed what to tell whom, and then set up a phone and food chain. Nora confirmed that Joe didn't want us to fuss over him or to be overly dramatic. As if we would!!!

"She said, 'He just wants your prayers.'

"I hate that! Just our prayers? What the hell? Praying is not enough action for me. I need to do more," I said then stood up abruptly.

"Anyway the surgery was this morning and I'm waiting for a call."

As I walked away, I heard the man on the park bench ask aloud, "Who was that woman?"

His wife said, "I thought you knew her. I hope Joe is okay."

51

How I Almost Saved a Mouse

My brother Joe is the second-most caring and generous person in my family. For years he and his wife Nora had a cottage in Ocean Grove, New Jersey, where every summer they would invite all of us, his nine siblings, to visit.

They gave us a place to stay; meals were a shared affair with us, the "guests," providing supplemental food and drinks and snacks.

Most of our siblings lived too far away to take Joe and Nora up on their kind offer, but Paul and I, and my sister Gretchen, would usually spend a few summer weekends with them.

One Friday Joe had to stay later than usual at work. He asked me to go to their house ahead of the others so I could empty the mousetraps scattered there. He said he'd had an exterminator in but was still finding the occasional rodent. I said, "Sure, no problem," and went early.

I only found one mouse. Alive, he was stuck to a trap which had a sticky-gluey surface. Mice would try to run across it and get stuck, and, I would guess, die, by starving to death.

NOT ON MY WATCH!

I took the little mouse outside, still stuck to the trap. I gently lifted each paw from the glue, and when all four were free, put him on the grass, and said the equivalent of "Vaya Con Dios." He didn't move. His paws must still have been a tad sticky. I gently pushed his little rear and, I think, he finally realized he was free, as he started to leave.

BAM! Out of nowhere a large russet-colored cat jumped him and ate him.

When I told Joe what had happened, he just shook his head.

Gret said, "So, I'm guessing, no mouse funeral today?"

Nora, on the other hand, was sympathetic and got me some lemonade.

Try to imagine Joe and Nora's insane summer weekends with me and my other siblings, as most of us would have done the same thing for the mouse.

Why is Joe the second-most caring and generous person in the family?

Because his wife Nora is the first.

Mom and Me

My favorite memories of mom and me are those of my eighth grade to high school years when we made the school lunches together very early in the morning. She would tell me family stories, quiz me on my English homework, and give me the inside scoop on the heroines in the Bible. We both liked the poem "Come into the garden, Maude" by Alfred Lord Tennyson. And for a while I called her Maude. She enjoyed teasing me by quoting obscure lines from even more obscure works and asking me who said it? I very seldom got the answers right, but we had some good laughs at my attempts.

Mom had a vast wealth of knowledge and easily quoted from history, religion, music, literature, theater, and of course the Bible. She peppered her everyday speech with casual references to the aforementioned:

"See those Christians how they love one another..."

"The quality of mercy is not strained..."

"The time has come, the walrus said..."

"How do I love thee? Let me count the ways..."

"A birdy with a yellow bill hopped upon my window sill..."

"The rosy mouth and rosy toes of little baby brother..."

"The child that is born on the Sabbath day..."

"The old order changeth, yielding place to the new. And God fulfills Himself in many ways..."

Mom was the one who told me that King Arthur's famous lines in *Idylls of the King* were directly quoted from the Bible and that people of his time were fully aware of this because they studied the Bible in all its richness as a work of literature as well as a source of religious inspiration.

I don't remember when I stopped getting up before six to be with Mom. Maybe this was a natural progression. I know at the time I was not aware of the precious gift I had been given. I am now.

An Emergency Meeting of the Family

We lined up, first by age, then by order of gang importance.

Apparently Dad had some big news.

"You're probably wondering why I called this meeting." He began.

"Not really," someone said, *sotto voce*. "We have one every Sunday night."

Our dad continued, as though he hadn't heard the remark. We all knew he had though because he had the sonar hearing of a bat.

"We are going to be moving." He continued. "To Ohio."

No one reacted. I think dad was disappointed by our lack of a response, but, we, his progeny, knew that we *never* went anywhere together. Church was attended in groups of three or four. At that time, we were attending five different schools: two were in two different grad schools, two were in college, two were in high school, and one was still in grammar school. The only thing that could ever get all of us headed to the same place, at the same time, was the promise of Dairy Queen coffee ice cream.

I could see each of my sibling's thoughts as though cartoonists were drawing dialogue bubbles over their heads.

Pat was thinking, "This could work. I could get my own room."

Mike was wondering if he would be able to drive in Ohio with his Connecticut learner's permit. Girls liked guys who could drive them places.

Sandie thought out loud, "Are the boys in Ohio cute?"

Chris was concerned that our two dogs and two cats might not be allowed in that Ohio place.

I was in love and my boyfriend was going to college in Connecticut, so Ohio held little allure for me.

Gretchen and Puss, who were both in the convent and just home visiting for the weekend, knew that family visits would be a thing of the past. Both of them had a somewhat pleased look on their faces.

Our mom was trying to appear supportive of the whole idea. But I knew she was dreading getting the house ready to put on the market, to say nothing of moving all of us and our grandmother, who was not a fan of change. Apparently our dad was going ahead to begin his new job while mom sold the house, packed us kids, and our belongings, and maintained the *status quo* while doing all of that.

Although we usually voted on big changes at family meetings, each of us knew this was a done deal. We were going to the Midwest, to a godforsaken state called Ohio.

What were our parents thinking?

In Illo Tempus Conceptus Bonus Erat

My mom hated what she called *rough housing*. That's what she called wrestling, pushing, shoving, biting, and bad manners. She had no sympathy for injuries incurred while rough housing. These could include cuts, scrapes, bruises, black eyes, and loose teeth. We would be told to *offer them up for the souls in purgatory*.

* * * * * * * * * * *

The floors in our kitchen were tile. This made for a slippery surface in winter. Picture on average six to eight pairs of boots tracking in clumps of snow and ice. I ran into the house and slipped. With my superior athletic skill, I hit the floor face first and split my chin open. My little sister Sandie followed me in, and, ever jealous of any attention I received, did the exact same thing. We had to go to the emergency room to be stitched up, but first, we had to clean up the blood and slush that was all over the place.

* * * * * * * * * * *

One time I got a deep cut on my right hand that required nineteen stitches. When my mom saw it, she asked *me* to drive us both to the hospital. She realized I needed something to distract me from a thumb cut through to the bone. I was fourteen at the time and did not have a driver's license.

* * * * * * * * * * *

In my family, there was a certain *je ne sais quoi* afforded one who had an injury, especially if a cast, or lots of blood, was involved. In my childhood, I had a few *je ne sais quoi*-s. When I got to high school and my French teacher translated the phrase, I was disappointed to learn it didn't mean "One who is amazing and brave."

* * * * * * * * * * *

A tomboy, I was always willing to try something physically challenging. Sometimes my big ideas didn't work out for me, or for my siblings. When this happened, my dad would show off and say something in Latin, like, "*In illo tempus conceptus bonus erat.*"

(Loosely translated, this means, it seemed like a good idea at the time.)
I hated Latin and usually my dad when he said stuff like that.

* * * * * * * * * * *

The best remedy for an ailment or injury is to have loved ones nearby. To be fair, sometimes my loved ones were there in the hospital with me because I had talked them into trying something really stupid and dangerous but which had seemed like a good idea at the time.

My Inheritance

"May I have your autograph, Mr. Churchill?"

No matter how many times my grandfather was asked to sign a book, a napkin or a piece of clothing, he was unfailingly cordial and willing. Perhaps that was because he was not Sir Winston Churchill. He just greatly resembled him.

*****

My great aunt Nell was full of self-importance. Knowing of the many lawyers, doctors, and businessmen in the family in Lancaster County, Pennsylvania, the Brubakers, Tuckers, and Allens, she decided to trace the family lineage back a few generations. She got as far as the four Brubaker brothers who were notorious horse thieves. She then declared, "What matters is not where you come from, but what you make of yourself."

*****

A young, handsome man, my dad was basking in the sun at Jones Beach, NY, when a mean bully kicked sand in his face. My younger siblings, new to the story, gaped at their formidable father. Who would dare to do that? (More to the point, our father, handsome?)

"What happened then, Dad?" anxiously queried Chris, the youngest of my nine siblings, who should have known better.

My dad grinned. "I married her."

*****

When Uncle Gene died, our fiery, intrepid Aunt Dot seemed, uncharacteristically, to be at a loss. She, who had visited Viet Nam on her own when she was in her mid-seventies, asked our mom if our family could help her with the detritus of a life cut short. We cooked meals, helped clear out their apartment, and acted as general dogs' bodies.

My brother Mike brought out a few of Uncle Gene's suits, asking Dot which one she wanted him to bring to the mortuary? And, just like that, the Dot we knew and loved was back!

59

"Good Heavens!" she admonished. "I'm not wasting a perfectly good suit by burying it. He came into the world naked; he can go out the same way."

At the funeral Mass, my sister Sandie had the happy task of reading from the Book of Job. When she got to the line, "Naked I came from my mother's womb," our entire family lost it. We were seen to be weeping into handkerchiefs and in each other's arms, shoulders shaking silently. Many were gratified by our obvious grief and love for Uncle Gene.

*****

I got my love of music and my smile from my mother, my sense of humor and my good looks from my father, and my most treasured inheritance – the stories of our family – from both of them.

S & H Green Stamps, Popsicles, and Puss

It happens in every family. A child will do something clever or goofy, or in my case certifiably insane, and a new name will attach itself to that hapless individual. Called a nickname, it becomes a part of the fabric of a family's life quilt. I didn't know my brother Moe's real name was Paul until I was ten years old.

Actually, I began this with the idea of telling my sister Mary Ellen's story. Moe's just came out of the blue. Mary Ellen's nickname is "Puss." It's terrible, I know, but by the time I came along, it was inscribed in stone.

One day Sandie, Mike, Pat, and I heard our Mom calling up the stairs. She used the words "Mary Ellen!" This was not a good thing. As we all know, a mother only calls a child by his proper name when there is trouble. One time my mom called me "Joan Mary" and I was grounded for a week. And it wasn't even my fault. Well, not totally. Anyway, the four of us crept down the stairs to hear about the terrible thing our big sister had done.

Puss is the best of the best of us. That she might have done something wrong shook and intrigued us.

Our mom had been distracted ever since our house had become infested with thousands of bugs. The exterminators had just departed and now she had to deal with her best, nicest, child's wrongdoing? This was powerful stuff.

As it turned out, Puss's latest project was the source of the infestation problem. Popsicle, the company that made our favorite frozen fruit treat, was running a program similar to the S & H Green stamp one our mom loved. If an individual collected 1,000 used Popsicle wrappers, that lucky child would get a new bike.

We kids knew about this because we were all helping Puss reach that goal. She would tie the wrappers in bundles of fifty and keep them in her desk. The latest count was over 700! She was going to win that bike and probably let us ride it.

Sadly, the exterminators, with our traitorous mother's permission, threw the offending, sugar-laden, bug-covered, sticky wrappers away.

"There was no joy in Mudville that day." Mighty Mary Ellen had struck out.

To be fair, we were getting a little sick of eating five Popsicles a day, but a bike, a new bike? That was worth the suffering. Not according to Mom, though.

Dad and Me

"They Also Serve Who Only Stand and Wait"

My dad was furious! I, who should have met his commuter train at 6:30 PM, pulled into the South Norwalk Station at 6:45. A sudden summer shower had soaked him as he waited umbrella-less on the platform.

He ripped open the driver's side door, rain dripping from the brim of his now ruined hat. The word "move" was barked. I moved.

During the half-hour drive home, he told me, "Remind me later to smack you."

I waited through supper and afterwards until he was having an after-dinner Scotch. I hovered silently at his left shoulder. After a lifetime, he turned towards me.

"Jonnie, what the hell are you doing?" he bellowed.

I said, "Dad, you told me to remind you to smack me."

He gaped at me, then waved me away with an imperious gesture.

"Go away," he said.

I went away.

Memories of Sandie

by her big sister Jonnie

small thin gap-toothed grin
little sister following following
running to catch up to the sister behind her
never realizing her musical brilliance
never noticing her uniqueness
silly silly taxi cab with the doors wide open
high school rebel long long hair
skinny skinny
playing piano painting with oils
ear infections more ear infections
a wealthy boyfriend *All their dishes match, Mom*
Ohio move so hard so hard
You're one of the Lanes aren't you?
chrysalis to butterfly in two short years
hearing aids gone I say HEARING AIDS GONE
a distance now popularity and pot
the sister I know but then again not
growing up and growing apart
damn
a wedding a bride a husband to love
a mother–to-be a mother-to-be a mother-to-be
when God when?
Niki *the heart that walks outside your body*
and time and time and time
so many states so many moves
Colorado again
the body the body it's falling apart
new hips soldered ankles electrified knees
a woman evolving weaker and stronger
a nest that's now empty a marriage bond severed
first steps to be taken again

small thin gap-toothed grin
little sister following following
older now poorer and richer
a woman who stands alone
taxi cab with the doors wide open
I'm sorry you're hurting
wanna make some fudge?

The Middle Child

Like Mary Poppins, Practically Perfect in Every Way

My First Confession and How I Learned All About Adultery

"There are many evils in this world." This I have known since my second grade "First Confession" when I had to confess my sins to a priest who was waiting for me in a shadowy box. A seven-year-old, I had a hard time coming up with any really terrible faults. I figured if I was going to be a sinner, I might as well be an interesting one.

I was pretty well versed in the Ten Commandments. My mother talked about them a lot, and I really loved the stories about Moses in the Bible. I especially liked when Moses asked God to have his brother Aaron lead the Israelites because he (Moses) "was slow of speech." Why, I asked myself, would he give up a chance to be the boss of an entire nation of Chosen People just because he talked slowly?

But I digress.

I was having a problem with the sixth commandment. I wasn't sure what "adultery" was, so I asked Sister Anita. I think she wasn't sure of what it meant either because she got that funny look on her face that she would get whenever I asked her a question. She finally told me it was "acting like an adult, but in a way that was not nice."

Now, in our attic there were lots of old clothes, including my great-grandmother's wedding dress. It was really neat because it had a slight bustle in the back, so it was the cause of many an argument as to who got to be the bride with the big butt. I figured fighting over an adult's wedding dress was probably committing adultery…

Father Francis McGuire was the lucky priest who got to hear my first confession. Imagine a childish voice admitting, with a certain relish, that its owner had committed adultery three times. He got up from his chair in the dark phone-booth-sized confessional and opened the curtain to the place where I knelt with great piety and sorrow for my sins.

"Hello, Jonnie," he said.

There's an "A" In Breast

When I was thirteen, my best friend in the whole world was a girl named Lillian. She had naturally curly hair, a bosom, and her own room. I envied her all three of those assets, but mostly her own room.

Lillian's room was perfection. The walls, drapes, and carpeting were all variations of the color purple. She had her own bed, her own desk, and her own dressing table with a skirt and a large mirror.

My room was terrible. I had an ugly old cherry bed which I had to share, a bow front dresser which I had to share, and a faded Persian rug which was the last word in U-G-L-Y. My adolescent heart pined for wall-to-wall purple.

But color wasn't the only thing my room lacked. It also lacked privacy. I would be writing the secrets of my soul in my diary and Sandie would saunter into our room. She'd look over my shoulder and say, "There's an 'a' in breast."

Then we would have a fight. We would divide our room down the middle and I couldn't step on her side and she couldn't step on my side. We would wake each other, if, in our sleep, one of us crossed the line we had drawn on the headboard of the bed. Sandie would wake up early and make her side of the bed while I was still sleeping. Of course, when I woke I would have to make the whole bed, which kept me pretty angry. So I wouldn't let her wear her blouse because it was on my side of the closet, which made her pretty angry...

Left to our own devices, Sandie and I would be fighting still, but my mother would eventually intervene with some Biblical quote like, "See those Christians, how they love one another." We wouldn't get what she meant by the quote, but her tone of voice was always easy to understand. It said, "Cut it out, you two."

We'd have to erase the chalk lines that were all over the room, promise not to be mean to each other, promise to respect each other's privacy, and shake hands. And for a while things wouldn't be too bad. Then I'd see a letter from Sandie's boyfriend sticking out from under her pillow...

Poor Lillian, her wall-to-wall lilac carpeting paled in comparison to the thrill of reading Sandie's drippy love letter aloud, at the top of my lungs, from the safety of a locked bathroom.

Scull Nixes Head of High School Paper

As my junior year in high school drew to a close, two things were sure things. One was that I would be the editor of the school paper my senior year, the other was that I would be the editor of the school paper my senior year.

Unfortunately, an error in judgment ended any chances of my ever wearing the coveted eyeshade. Our principal, a kind elderly man, died of a heart attack and a young dynamic priest named Father Scull was appointed to take his place. Obviously, this was front-page news.

The newspaper staff had had a long afternoon putting the paper to bed. We were all a little punchy as we tried to finish up the last few headlines. One by one, the kids began to leave as their parents arrived to pick them up. Sister Winifred had long since gone over to the convent, and our numbers had dwindled to two hardy souls.

We split the remaining headlines and worked with a will. Lillian finished hers and went to her locker to get her books. I was struggling with the article on the two principals when the perfect words flashed before my eyes. I wrote them down, and, lucky me, they weren't a bad fit. I wrote: CENTRAL LOSES HEAD, SCULL TAKES OVER! I typed it up and left it on the pile for Sister Winifred to check in the morning.

Need I go on? Sister Winifred didn't check our work as carefully as was her wont. The headline was there in the galleys when they were returned, and it cost the school some coins to change it. It also cost me the editorship. And guess who couldn't wait to meet me his first day on the job?

It was a long senior year.

"At Last, Exquisite Columbine, I Have Vanquished My Rivals ..."

Acting is not my thing. It never has been, nor will it ever be. That being said, when I was twenty, my senior year in college, some friends begged me to take a "small" role in a one-act play competition they were entering. When I read the part I was to have, I agreed at once. I had one line and had to do two things: walk on stage and fall at the feet of the heroine, Columbine.

I memorized my "line" and began practicing falling. I fell backwards, sideways, and forwards. I slipped, tripped, and tumbled until I was black and blue. None of my falls were what the directors had in mind, so they decided to write the action out of the script.

For our opening, and closing, night I wore a pair of too-large-for-me boots and a black velvet cloak which was a tad too long. I went to sweep grandly on stage and stepped on the cape. Dancing a frenetic boogie while trying to regain my balance, I slid across the stage and landed on my back, at the "Star's" feet, exactly where I should have been according to the original stage direction, except that my head was under her floor-length skirt. I was mortified. She was mortified. I lifted the hem of her gown, spoke my line and let it fall again.

Everybody was furious with me. My buddies were convinced I'd done it on purpose. The "Star" was convinced I was part of some dastardly plan to make her look terrible. And, to top it all off, I made the local paper because I was "such a natural comedic actress."

Things quieted down. We won the one-act play competition. After a while my friends began speaking to me again. The "Star" magnanimously forgave me, and my collegiate life continued. I'm glad I did the play. It was a learning experience. I learned humility, how to fall, and that I'm a "natural comedic actress."

"In the Spring A Young Man's Fancy..."

Every spring I drive Paul crazy by trying to get slim and gorgeous in two or three weeks' time. I do double exercise classes, start doing my hair and nails with extra care, and, in general, do what any woman with sense does all of the time.

The first hint that it was not working came the day I got my contact lenses. In all the old movies, yes, even on Broadway, when the rather plain secretary takes off her glasses, she suddenly has big boobs and a beautiful face. As soon as the lenses were in place, I checked my chest. Could Hollywood possibly have been wrong?

I used to run. I didn't run fast or especially well. I just did it. At that time, I didn't have contact lenses. I would run with my glasses on until they became foggy, then I would carry them and run a lot more carefully. I am very near-sighted. In my travels down the Boulevard without glasses, I have run into a boy on a moped, a girl carrying a French horn, and a three-foot high, three-foot wide rock painted green to resemble a frog. My neighbors signed a petition to keep me off the streets, and I gracefully retired.

I also did a stint with aerobics, which I loved. But the thrifty Yankee in me, who rarely surfaces, felt guilty paying money to do what I could be doing on my own for free. Actually, it wasn't the class that was expensive; it was the outfits I felt compelled to wear. I couldn't shame my family by looking tacky while I exercised, could I?

Back at square one, I stand in front of my mirror and sigh. If beauty is truly in the eye of the beholder, then I wish my beholder's eyes were as near-sighted as mine are.

Joan of Arc, St. Theresa, and Me

In parochial school we were often told stories about the lives of the saints. St. Theresa, The Little Flower, advocated a life of doing small acts of goodness and kindness every day. She died of Tuberculosis when she was twenty-four.

St. Joan of Arc, on the other hand, rode a horse, told the Dauphin, the Prince of France, what to do, and actually went into battle. She was later burned at the stake.

You can imagine, my being ten and all, which kind of saint I wanted to be.

My mom, after hearing me loudly declaring which saint I was going to be, usually while I was brandishing a stick sword and yelling the only French words I knew which were "Bon jour! Bon jour," tried to tell me that being good and kind and loving all of the time would be a difficult task indeed. She was probably thinking, "Especially for you, Jonnie." But I was resolute. Joan of Arc and I even had the same first name, for Pete's sake!

Older now and somewhat wiser, I see what my mother was trying to share with me. Leaping on a horse and saving France would be great. But doing the right thing day in and day out would be harder, much, much, harder.

Which brings me to my twenty-first-century self. Reading about a woman who drove her small children into a lake to let them drown while she escaped tested my ability to be compassionate and loving and forgiving.

And I failed the test. Even knowing she is now trying to make amends, I can't find it in my heart to forgive her. I'm thinking maybe sainthood may not be in the cards for me.

"It Ain't Me, Babe"

I'm tired. I'm so tired I can't even think. I got a part-time job nine days ago, and I think I'll die of old age before the first two weeks are up.

First of all, I am not organized. I thought I was, but organized as a housewife is different from organized as a working woman. Which brings us to my second problem. I am used to dressing like "Jonnie the jock" or "Jonnie, Jim's mother," not "Jonnie the well-dressed working woman." My feet miss their sneakers, my body its sweats.

Then of course there are the odd incidentals like meals to be prepared, clothing to be ironed, bathrooms to be cleaned, and homework to be gone over. In time, I hope to do one out of the four per week.

And then there is the man I married. I don't know how long he is going to go along with a wife who can't keep her eyes open after eight, to say nothing of having her arms open to him. I'm beginning to realize what the phrase "the spirit is willing, but the flesh is weak" actually means.

But I'm not going to give up without a fight. After all, it's only been nine days. Things could improve. In another week or two, I'll probably be able to stay up until nine. My feet will get used to three-inch heels, my bathrooms won't look so bad…

One thing I will never do again, though, is take for granted the efforts of my friends who work full time outside the home. Being a wife and mother is difficult and demanding. The woman who is both of these and a career woman, too, is someone very special. But she sure as hell isn't me.

No Woman Is an Island

Business trips are not my idea of a fun time. In fact they're right up there with liver on the list of things I can do without.

Whenever Paul went on a business trip, I stayed home with the kids and Jay Leno. For some reason, I can't seem to sleep when Paul is away. It's not that I'm afraid – it's just that I develop an amazing awareness of everything that lives and breathes within a two-mile radius of my home.

Usually I fill the sleepless hours with wild cleaning binges. I vacuum and polish and dust. I rearrange closets. I iron clothes I hate and never wear. Then I iron clothes the kids hate and never wear.

I miss him. The kids miss him. And I always mean to tell him so. But when he walks in the door, the adrenaline, which has kept me on a Mister Clean high for five nights, drains away, leaving me yawning hugely into the back of my hand just before I kiss him hello.

Fortunately, the kids cover for me, jumping all over him, half carrying, half dragging his bags into the house, nattering about all the things that happened while he was away.

Business trips of some sort have always been part of a working person's job. But when they become a part of my job and I'm not even in California or on the trip, I resent it.

I'm also resentful of the feelings of inadequacy they foster. Who wants to know she is one of the people John Donne wrote about? It seems as though I've always understood that "No man is an island." But "No woman is an island?" I hate it.

Skiing, Sport or Torture?

Everyone in my family took to skiing like a duck to water. Steph began when she was three. We put her on skis, told her to wave her arms up and down as though she were flying, and pushed her down the hill. She made it. I, on the other hand, who had poles, age, and athletic ability to get me down, made it about four yards before I became paralyzed from the neck up. My brain refused to accept that I would voluntarily place myself in such a situation.

No matter how many times I went skiing, it was always a battle to remember that I was having fun. To be fair to the sport, I would have to admit my beginning years in skiing were spent mostly on my knees, gloves off, helping whichever child Paul wasn't helping, fixing bindings, finding poles, brushing off snowsuits, etc. But Paul did all of that, too, and he still loves it.

Be that as it may, there evolved around New Year's Day the tradition that the Garstka Family would go skiing. In the beginning, it was only Paul and Jim who would get up at 5 AM the first day of the New Year and drive off laden with food, maps, and equipment. Then Gretchen joined them, and I watched in panic as my excuses for not going dwindled.

New Year's Day had somehow become a mid-winter's Mother's Day for me. On New Year's Eve, I would bake and wrap and pack the food and provisions for the skiers. New Year's Day, I would have the house to myself. I could do the post-Christmas cleaning, or I could hit the sauna at the tennis club, or I could build a fire and read all day. My only responsibility was to have some homemade soup and bread ready when the ravenous skiers returned.

When Steph finally joined the rest of the gang on their outing, Paul tried to convince me to join them. He felt I was staying home because I was trying to spare the family budget the added expense of another adult skier. It's very humbling when someone attributes higher motives to your actions than are true. I just wanted to be by myself for a day.

An only child, Paul was often lonely. Because of his childhood, he hates to leave me alone because he thinks I will feel lonely too. I grew up with wall-to-wall family. I don't remember ever feeling lonely. I love my family very much. I love them even more after a day away from them.

So, this year, I'll bake their favorite apple cake, peel the carrots and celery, put together huge roast beef sandwiches, stuff the backpack with chips and fruit, and happily wave them all off. They'll come back loaded with stories of their ski adventures and I, relaxed and refreshed, will enjoy hearing them.

The Expert and The Screw Up

There's a lady on my street who has all the answers. You don't even have to ask her for advice; she gives it for free. She knows teenagers. She's an expert because she was once a teenager herself. Her kids try to tell her things, but she is too smart to listen to them. Her husband tries to show her another point of view but, since hers is always the right one, she can't be bothered to listen. She insisted on giving a party for her kids. She baked and cleaned and brought out her best things because she knew best. She wasn't one of those adults who buy or serve kids beer or wine. Oh, no, she just gave them her house and the opportunity to drink their own with impunity and anonymity. When her house was made a mess, when fights broke out, when her neighbors were subjected to foul language and loud music, when her yard was littered with cigarettes, beer bottles, and vomit, she had no one to blame but herself.

The lady was way off base. Hopefully she's learned a lesson. Her husband, who had been on a business trip, told her, "So, we learned something. Real education never comes cheap." Sounds like a great guy to me.

I've got to go. I have to recycle some beer and wine cooler bottles.

You see, there was a party at my house…

I don't want to talk about it.

The Best Comeback Ever

For me, writing was never the problem. Not a strong arguer as a child, I would retreat to my room after losing a verbal battle of wits with one of my nine mean, horrid siblings and demolish him or her with brilliant, albeit written, retorts.

In person, when challenged, I would come back with such rapier sharp witticisms as "Oh, yeah?" Or, my personal favorite, "Says you." But with my trusty pen and legal pad, I could annihilate them all. I would return downstairs and look upon them with pity…

Fast-forward thirty-five years to a confrontation on the Cape Cod Rail Trail. Bridget, my Golden Retriever puppy, and I are walking on the bike path. It is six fifteen in the morning and we think we are alone. So alone are we that I am talking aloud to her as though she can actually understand my humor and incredibly witty repartee.

A cyclist comes around one of the two bends on the entire Island of Cape Cod, and he and Bridget and I become entangled in Bridget's very long leash. As I repeatedly apologize, he repeatedly tells me "There's a reason why this route is called the "BIKE PATH.""

I, with the strong mental and verbal talents developed over the period of thirty years since my childhood, gently remind him that it is also called the 'Cape Cod Rail Trail'; that the path is for walkers as well as for cyclists and joggers, and that perhaps he could call out when coming around a path with an obstructed view.

Actually, that's what I wish I'd said. What I did do was apologize over and over again as he peddled away. And when he was far enough away that he couldn't possibly hear me, I yelled out, "Oh, yeah?" And "Says you!"

"A Wind Is in The Heart of Me ..."

Yesterday I went for a jog on the Boulevard and I was struck by the vast difference in my life and in me since my last run. When my children were at home, running was a form of escape, a means of letting off steam, a precious time of silence. I ran to keep my weight down and my stamina up.

Now I'm an 'empty nester.' The kids have long since begun their adult lives, and Paul and I are alone at last. My reasons for getting and staying in shape are very different. Now I run with joy, simply because I still can. I work out to maintain and preserve flexibility, vitality, and the right to have an ice cream cone once in a while. I want to keep step with Paul, not take him in two out of three falls.

Do I run every day? Heck no. My knees couldn't take that kind of a beating. I play tennis, some very bad golf, and on occasion hard-to-get. Paul and I do our own gardening and yard work and congratulate ourselves on a daily basis for the wisdom we showed in buying a hot tub.

Back on the Boulevard, I run sometimes, walk sometimes, talk to strangers most times, and in general have a good time. I'm where I want to be for now. I can feel my second wind beginning to rise. Where will it take me? I have no idea, but this time has given me the chance to get ready.

So has the Boulevard.

Husbands,
They Can
Be Trained.

The Rules

In our family there are rules. These have been made clear to our children, who, whether they accept them or not, know them well. One such dictate is about tattoos and the consequences a family member would face should he or she get one. I believe the threats covered non-payment for orthodontia, college tuitions, and weddings, but there could have been more. With this preface in mind, I give you this family story.

Paul's idea was a good one. He wanted to take our family to a sunny vacation spot, away from the "Madding Crowd," so we could all reconnect with each other. Jim and Gretchen had both graduated from their respective colleges and were each not only gainfully employed and living on their own, but also in loving relationships. Steph, a senior in college, was also headed toward adulthood, independence, and her own place. This trip would be our last chance to vacation alone together as the *fab five* we have been for twenty-two years.

It was our first St Martins' beach day and Jim was behaving oddly. I was concerned about the distance he seemed to need to be from the rest of us and decided to do something about it. I called out to him as he was walking away, yet again.

"Jim, wait up," I shrilled.

He turned reluctantly, impatiently.

"Honey, what's wrong?" I asked. Then continued before he could speak. "Listen, I know you smoke. You know my feelings about it, but that is your decision. So come on back to the rest of the family and be with us and smoke."

He sighed and turned around. Wrenching open his Don Johnson Miami Vice shirt, he exposed his chest and stomach.

"It's this," he said.

I looked.

"So, you've gained some weight. Everybody does in college. You'll lose it. I'm sure."

"No!" he exclaimed. "This!"

I looked closer. *This* was what looked like a blurred number sign the size of a silver dollar high on his left breast.

"What is it?" I asked.

"It's the Japanese symbol for creativity," he explained.

"What, like a tattoo?" I asked curiously.

"Yes! A tattoo. A tattoo!" he rejoined, shouting a bit.

"Ooooh," I echoed, relief obvious in every long vowel sound.

He exploded with frustration.

"That's it? I haven't taken my shirt off in front of you and Dad for three years, and this is your reaction???"

"Well," I considered, lips pursed. "Go show your father. I'm pretty sure he will have something to say about it."

With an exclamation of disgust, Jim turned around and headed back toward his father who was attempting to body surf and not doing well. I watched the two of them meet, talk, and surf together. Then Jim commandeered his younger sister, Stephanie, and they went off together to shop at one of the ubiquitous thatched huts that dotted the shoreline. Paul came out of the water and walked toward me.

"How did you and Jim do?" I asked.

"Really well," he replied. "Whatever you said to him, it worked."

I smiled up at this dear man, my husband of forty years.

"So, what did you think of his tattoo?" I asked.

His response was immediate and incredulous.

"Jim has a tattoo?"

A Funny Thing Happened ...

We had had a super New Year's Party and I was cleaning up the debris the next day. I took the large wreath, which had had the place of honor on our glass coffee table and threw it into the fireplace. A lighted match soon took care of the wreath and my lovely white living room walls. I forgot to open the flue.

Paul was testy when he came in and saw the mess I'd made. Huge smoky grey streaks rose from both sides of the hearth. The mantle was blistered and sooty, and the room was full of smoke.

"You made the mess," he said. "You clean it up."

Fair enough. I got to work. The room soon aired out. I washed the windows, the walls, and the mantle. I polished the furniture and vacuumed the rug. Everything came beautifully clean, except the walls and mantle. The long, finger-like marks were still there for all to see.

So I got my trusty ladder and brushes and paint and painted over the marks. The wall looked brand new. At least it did until Paul came home from work. He looked at it and then called me into the room. I couldn't believe my eyes. The marks had re-appeared. "You'll have to paint it again," he said.

The next day, I painted the area again. Now, it really looked super. I called Paul at work and said, "Not to worry, Honey. This time it really looks great." But when we looked at the wall that night, the marks had re-appeared again.

Paul stepped back from the hearth and put his hand up to scratch his head in puzzlement. His wrist hit the chandelier, which gently turned in a circle. As the pendant light moved, so did the scorch marks. Brilliant person that I am; I had been trying to paint the shadows cast by the light of the chandelier. Of course the wall looked clean during the day. It was clean. The shadows only appeared at night when the light was turned on.

Paul was a good sport about the whole thing. He turned around, bent over, and said, "Go ahead. Kick me."

Of course, I didn't. I just wish he'd give me another shot at it now.

Out and About Inside Out

Last summer, days of soaring temperatures and high humidity caused me to change the time I took our Golden Retriever, Bridget, for her morning constitutional. Seven is our normal departure time. This particular day, we walked at 5:30. And, although I consider myself a morning person, I'll admit I wasn't operating on all four cylinders.

Paul, who was also up early, looked at me and said, "Nice shirt." As the item in question was new, I said, "Thanks," thinking it was a compliment, and walked out. My new shirt was inside out, and obviously so, with its dark seams and stitching, wrongfully, glaringly apparent.

After a nice, cool, long walk, Bridget and I got takeout at the Blueberry Muffin, picked up the mail, and dropped off some dry cleaning.

I thought people were smiling at me more than they usually do, but no one mentioned my inside out-ness.

I finally realized what I had done as I was walking down to the lake behind Great Island in the Pinehills. I looked forward. I looked back. I saw no one. I then switched my shirt to its rightful outside out place in the world of clothing.

I should have looked up. A man, who had been working on the sprinkler heads in his back yard, which was a story above me, grinned and saluted me.

Initially, I thought, "There are no words …" But when I got back home, I managed to find a few for Paul.

Tennyson's Brook and Paul

I was waiting at the New York Marathon's twenty-five-mile marker. Paul was going to run by any second now, and I was going to take a super picture, which I would then have made into a huge poster.

Of course he didn't know this because it was going to be one of his birthday presents. I babbled on and on like Tennyson's Brook to my friends Nell and Anne about this and that while we waited and waited and waited.

I looked over my shoulder, away from the course, and there he was! My first thought was that he'd done it, qualified for Boston! And I'd been so busy yacking, I'd missed him and the picture. Then I saw his face.

The kids hadn't seen him. It was just Paul and me. He didn't have an "it-doesn't-matter" look on yet. All those months of five A.M. runs, the Sunday twenty-mile endurance tests, the hours of running alone, had come to this: a rare, humid, 80-degree day in late October, and a marathon he couldn't finish.

I wanted to hold him and rock him and love him, but I didn't. I just got him his clothes and some water. But I think he knew.

Paul ran the New York Marathon four times. His best time was 3:15; his worst, the time he didn't finish. It's funny. The kids only remember that one.

He Loves Me, He Loves Me Not

Valentine's Day was like a breath of fresh air. Everyone was in love – at least for the day, and winter's hold didn't seem to be as tight as it had been. The kids gave and received their cards, flowers, and candies, and Paul went on a trip to Tennessee.

As each of the kids came in from school, I was asked, "What did Dad get you this year, Mom?"

Their dad never forgets anything, especially an event like Valentine's Day. I've gotten everything from new jogging sneakers, nighties and flowers, to tennis rackets, flannel sheets, and a pasta-making machine. Except for this year. He forgot.

The kids were upset with Paul. I tried to explain the things he did remember to do...like split and pile the firewood on the deck so we wouldn't have to go out in the snow to get it...like filling up the gas tanks in both cars...like leaving cash on the windowsill for emergencies (such as Pizza Kings). But they were unconvinced. They thought I was covering for him.

When I was their age(s), I wouldn't have bought it either. At fourteen, true romance could only involve flowers, candy, candlelight, and a very attentive male. But the night before Paul went on his trip, he took me to the mall. He didn't want to go shopping; I did. So we went. We were there for several hours. I was happy. He wasn't, but he let me do 'my thing.' Thoughtfulness, like that, means more to me than a phone call to FTD and a quick charge on a credit card.

Besides, he called me after the kids were in bed, and he's coming home tonight.

Don't drop by. I'll be busy.

Basketball, Dads, and Legends

The purpose of the exercise was to toughen Jim up. He and Paul were going over to the high school to see if they could get in on a pick-up game of basketball. From the way my two men were talking, I gathered most of the guys playing would be either seniors or recent graduates. As a five-foot-ten, 135-pound freshman, Jim stood a pretty good chance of getting clobbered. But I was just a mother, what did I know?

I tried to make it clear to Paul that I would be less than pleased if my son got killed in a basketball game after I had safely gotten him through Measles, Chicken Pox, and learning how to cross the street. With a smile and a hug, Paul assured me that all would be fine, and they took off.

The phone call came close to ten o'clock. "Hi, Mom? It's Jim. We're at the hospital. No, no, I'm fine, Mom. It's Dad. He got hit in the mouth and the doctor says he'll need five or six stitches."

They came in together with the most self-satisfied look I've ever seen on either face. Paul's mouth was packed with gauze. It had to hurt him to smile. But smile he did. The two of them were celebrating, as only the male of the species can, with "high fives" and shoulder punches.

That did it! All of a sudden, I was angry! I was all set to send Jim to the showers when he blurted out what a star his dad had been. The other team was losing and, in their anger, got a little rough. "The guy who nailed Dad did it on purpose, Mom. Dad got mad and wouldn't stop playing. We won by one hoop, and guess who made it?"

Jim went to bed that night, convinced his father was a legend in his own time. I was up that night with the legend, getting him aspirin, ice, and liniment.

Who would have thought legends would be so vulnerable and so lovable?

Gas and Diesel Fuel, How Different Can They Be?

Many years ago, I was making dinner when Paul came lurching into the kitchen. His face was black, his clothing reeked of gasoline and oil, his eyes were squeezed tightly shut, as in a hoarse voice he croaked, "How do I look"?

Unaware of the undercurrents of high drama, I said, "On a scale of one to ten? About a two."

He opened his eyes long enough to glare at me and repeated himself. "I mean, how is my face?"

Looking closer this time, I could see that his eyebrows and eyelashes were gone, as was a good deal of his hair.

But let me back up a little. The car in Paul's life at that time was a '59 Mercedes. He loved to work on it, rebuilding the engine, repairing the bodywork, etc., etc. I was very seldom allowed to drive this wonder. Unfortunately, one of the few times I did, I let it run out of gas. To add insult to injury, with the help of a very authoritative male of the species, I put diesel fuel in a non–diesel car.

It went maybe three yards, gasped, and then died a horrible death. I had to be towed three miles to the tune of thirty dollars, and Paul had to siphon all of the diesel fuel from the car's gas tank. Small wonder that he was not all sweetness and light when a spark from the industrial vacuum he was using ignited the gas/diesel mixture that was all over him.

But that was many years ago. Paul's eyebrows and eyelashes returned, as did his hair. After a fashion, we got back on a first name basis. The Mercedes was sold.

Now another car holds the place of honor in the garage. I'll go out to announce the fact that dinner is ready and two blackened faces will appear from underneath the chassis. Time was, time is.

As a matter of fact, last night at the dinner table I asked the men in my life when could I take the Porsche out for a spin? Two horrified male voices, at the same time, chorused, "Not yet!"and "Never!"

I think men get overprotective when it comes to their cars.

There's Something About a Man with Scars

Here I am back in a hospital waiting room, this time waiting for my husband Paul. With the removal of the torn cartilage in his left knee, he will have achieved a matched set. I keep telling him I love a man with seams, but I don't think he believes me.

He sees his scars as some sort of denegation of the man he once was. I see them as medals of valor.

He broke his hand keeping the kids' toboggan from wrapping itself around a tree. He broke his nose in a father-daughter soccer game. He tore the cartilage in his right knee in a father-son soccer game. And he got six stitches in the mouth because of a pick-up basketball game he and Jim were in.

Those of you who are astute, darn you, will notice I haven't mentioned any wife-related injuries. I once got Paul so angry with me he put his fist through a door. It still swells in damp weather. The fist, I mean; the door we replaced. And I already mentioned the time his eyebrows and eyelashes were burned off because of my stupid mistake.

There can't be too many families that have as many tangible signs of their father's love as we do. There is a tremendous security that comes from being loved like this. We're very lucky.

But poor Paul! His love for us is going to kill him.

About Opposites Attracting ...

I know the phrase "mixed marriage" is not politically correct, or correct, in any way, but my husband Paul and I embody the concept. I am one of ten children. He is an only child.

I am a throw away-er. He is a saver. He has a type-A personality. I am nowhere to be found on that particular scale. I am right brained. He is left brained.

I relish being alone. To Paul, to be alone is to be lonely.

I'm tired of sharing. I've shared responsibility, hairbrushes, and blame all of my life. Paul is happy to share and is always surprised when I growl at his fork as it nears my mashed potatoes, piece of pie, etc.

Paul likes to shop. A hardware store outing will keep him smiling for days. Ten minutes into Home Depot and my eyes are rolling back in my head.

I love change. I would stage our house a different way every week if I could. Paul doesn't understand this. Why would I again move furniture that he has already helped me move four or five or six times???

He prefers to be cautious; I am a risk taker. His line of work is finance. He loves numbers, Sudoku, budgets, and lists. I used to teach high school English. I find words fascinating. The New York Times crossword puzzle can amuse me for days.

He's an Independent. I am a Democrat. Enough said.

He has never had a food fight. I never started a food fight but was happy to join in when one of my teammates tagged me. Paul never had to share clothing. I was the happy recipient of the outgrown outfits of three older sisters. One Easter, my dad had the brilliant idea of getting all six of us girls the same coats and hats. Five years later, I was still wearing that coat; well, Gretchen's, then Ginger's, then Mary Ellen's. My poor sister Pat, the youngest of the six of us, is still wearing it.

At a party, if the hostess announces that dinner is ready, Paul will finish his sentence. I, on the other hand, am already seated, napkin in lap, fork in hand.

If Paul walks into a room, the TV will immediately be on. If he is working on a project, the radio will too. That's not to say, I don't like to watch television or listen to tunes, but noise is another thing that abounded in my early years. So, I don't mind silence.

Directions? Let's talk about them. He reads them. I do too, but only as a last resort. And as for a sense of direction, Paul has a gyroscope in his head. You could put a blindfold on him, twirl him around four times, and he could still find true north. I once got lost in a deep linen closet.

As poles apart as we seem to be, we do share the same faith, the same sense of humor, the same work ethic, and the same love of family. With nine siblings, I had a wonderful support system when our parents were ill and needed us. I never had the sole responsibility for my parents in their old age the way Paul has had. He is amazing and loving and unselfish. I think people sometimes assume that members of a large family are more giving and generous because they had to be those things in order to survive. Not so, at least not in my case. Anytime I could duck behind a sibling, I did. And when there was work, to be done, I was pretty good at disappearing.

So, I'm not Patricia Perfect and he's not Gandhi. Yet somehow it works. Not all the time. In fact he's pretty mad at me now. And that's another place where we differ. I'll forget we're fighting and ask him if he wants a glass of wine. He can stay annoyed for two or three days. Poor guy, he still thinks the silent treatment will bother me. Hello?

Our Papa, Paul's father, often says, "The first forty-five years of marriage are the hardest." This year, Paul and I will meet this milestone. If Papa is right, things should be smooth sailing from now on. Hmmm…

Empty Nest

It's not so bad this empty nest, just you and me again.
We'll have more time, just you and me,
to be lovers instead of just friends
Sometimes I didn't listen. The kids' needs got in the way.
Sometimes I was too tired to love. "You think you had a bad day?"
But things will be different now
It's not so bad this empty nest, just you and me again.
We'll do things together, just you and me,
antiquing and tennis and Zen.
I'll go to the places you go, sit in on a card game or two
You can come to my Pilates class, have your hair colored, too
Boy, things will be different now.
It's driving me nuts, this empty nest, just you and me again,
I have no space, you're always here, and I can't stand your friends
We've grown into different people.
Our interests aren't always the same.
Our minds, horizons, and bodies have changed.
This isn't some Newlywed Game.
Yes, things are different now.
Now I love you, truly love you, as only maturity can.
It's more than your eyes, the sound of your voice,
your gently caressing hand.
I love you the father, I love you the son,
I love you my husband, my lover
We've worlds of experience yet to explore,
so many things to discover.
And things will be different now.
Yes, things will be different now.
Boy, things will be different now.

Children:

Why When There are Plants?

Jim

A curious child, Jim was always asking me difficult-to-answer questions, like "Is there a rock in my knee?" or "Why don't girls have a penis?" When he was five, he told me he had a headache. Running my hand over his tussled blond hair, I asked, "Where does it hurt, honey?" He answered, "In my stomach."

Ever an athlete, I learned just how good he was when I came upon him escaping from his crib. No cautious exit was this. He literally vaulted over the side barricade. Needless to say, we left the gate down from then on, and bought him a big boy bed the following weekend.

Jim has also, always, had a soft spot when it comes to his family. Only eighteen months older than Gretchen, he was ever her protector.

One time when Gretchen was six months old, she began to cry and I, in Jim's opinion, was not quick enough to go to see what the matter was. When the crying abruptly stopped, however, my mother's radar kicked in and I hustled to their shared bedroom. Jim was standing there, his arm inserted between the slats of Gretchen's crib. She was busily, happily, sucking on his thumb. He glared at me as if to say, "Don't say a word, just don't say a word."

A brave big brother, Jim had to take on the neighborhood bad boy when he pushed Gretchen face down in the sandbox. Jim jumped on Eddie and fought a valiant albeit losing battle against him. Then, in the way of boys, they became friends. Gretchen lived.

Another time, when we were living in Rochester, NY, Jim and Paul built a fabulous luge run in our back yard. We lived on a long hill, so this took some masterful planning and engineering, things both of my men loved to do. After the sides were built up and the snow tamped down, six-year-old Jim had the great idea of pouring water on the run so that, overnight, it would turn to ice and make for an even better, faster sledding run. His father, the idiot, agreed and they iced their project down. The first child, after Paul, to try out the ice tunnel was little Jenny Smith, who fell down and broke her arm. I'm not even sure Jim ever got to try it out. Both guys still insist it was a great idea and that Jenny ruined everything.

I love Jim best because, although he shares his left side of the brain gifts, his blue, blue eyes, and his ability to fix anything with his father, he has my sense of humor. Athletic, funny, sensitive, intelligent, and kind, Jim is a wonderful person. He's a lot like me.

Gretchen

"Can I have a nickel, Dad?" It was Gretchen, her face alight with anticipation and fun.

"Why do you need a nickel?" her father asked.

Dancing from one foot to the other with impatience at the question, she replied, "Because some kids from up the street are selling rocks!"

Then there was the time we couldn't find her shoes. They were orthopedic, heavy, and ugly, and I empathized with Gretchen when she took them off, which was often. But they were also very expensive. We had to find them. Gretchen thought for a while and then remembered that she had left them at the house of the girl with the curly hair.

Up the hill and around the corner we walked, knocking on doors, ringing doorbells, asking the same question over and over. "Did Gretchen leave her shoes here?" The neighbors were all very nice but shoeless. Finally a woman answered the door, a little girl with curly hair clinging to her shorts. "Yes," she said. "Gretchen did leave her shoes here. I was just going to call you."

We were jubilant! While we were on our quest, Gretchen had mentioned her friend's bedspread with *blue* ducks. She had also told me about her nice dog. But she hadn't thought it worth mentioning that the curly haired girl was black.

One time while we were visiting John and Kay, our best friends from college, we decided to take a walk in the woods. We had our two little children with us. Jim was four and Gretchen was two and a half. Kay asked Gretchen what her favorite song was. Perched on Kay's shoulders, Gretchen answered. "*Country Girl*, do you want me to sing it?"

When a startled Kay replied, "Yes," Gretchen proceeded to sing the very long Olivia Newton John song, which has three verses and a repeating refrain. She hadn't finished by the time we got to John and Kay's house, and their faces were a study.

I love Gretchen best because although she is like Paul, beautiful, analytical, organized, and smart, she shares my love of music and animals. A loving, caring person, she's a lot like me.

Stephanie

Steph is the youngest of our three children. She had four days of peace in the hospital before she began her car-seat existence. Car pools to nursery school, carpools to dance classes, carpools to swimming lessons, and carpools to soccer, basketball, and baseball games.

Steph was the best baby. She thrived on activity, sudden loud noises, and peanut butter sandwiches. Calm, happy, cute as could be, she followed Jim and Gretchen wherever they went. In keeping up with them, she learned how to run, jump, swim, play soccer, and dance with a skill and style far beyond her tender years.

When Steph was two and a half, she discovered Halloween. Dressed as a bewhiskered gray mouse, she went door to door. Amazed that all she had to do was say was "Trick or Treat" and she would be given candy, she kept looking over her shoulder at me, checking my reaction to see if this was all on the up and up. Happily, it was. She fell asleep in the midst of her chocolate loot that night, a smile on her tired little face.

The next day I received a call from our neighbor, Mickey Smith. She was laughing as a she spoke. It seems a little girl wearing a gray mouse hat was making the rounds of the neighborhood again, ringing doorbells and saying, "Trick or Treat!"

By the time Steph arrived at Mickey's house, three doors down, she had a decent amount of candy. My neighbors, who were no help at all, thought she was so cute, they had all given her more.

From the beginning, Stephanie took care of her brother and sister. She would say things like: "Don't spank Jim, he didn't mean it," or "Gretchen's sorry now." The heart of the family, she is always the one who reminds us that it's time to get together again.

I love Stephanie best because she has her father's ability to be silent, his love of order, and his beautiful eyes. A lovely, honest, hardworking and loyal young woman, she's a lot like me.

Why Yes, I'll Chaperone

My job was a simple one. I had to lead a group of fifth graders into the Great Swamp and (hopefully) lead them back out, on the same day, in the same physical condition. Armed with a clearly marked map and a compass, we were going to do something called *orienteering*.

Fortunately for our group, my son Jim was with us. I say fortunately because even at the tender age of eleven he was aware of his mother's total lack of a sense of direction. While the other fifth graders crowded around me, listening to every pearl of woodsy wisdom that fell from my lips, Jim was busy, cutting notches in trees, and shredding his clothing, leaving a corduroy trail behind us.

Our first compass points were to bring us to a tree split by lightning. We didn't find the tree. Can you believe we were in a well-forested swamp and we couldn't find a tree?

Our second check point, according to the map, was an unusual rock formation. We didn't find that either. We did, however, find water…in our shoes, in our pants' cuffs, in our sandwiches.

Our third and final objective was to return to the compass markings, which pinpointed the lodge where all this good learning fun had begun. When our group finally stumbled onto the parking lot a block away from the lodge, I figured we were close enough.

That school trip was most educational. I learned many new things. Perhaps the most enlightening of which was the fact that the average fifth-grade American male can be bought. A quick side trip on the way back to school, ice cream for everyone, and their lips were sealed.

I fear for the future.

The Role of Mary

When Gretchen was in third grade, our church decided to put on a Christmas Pageant. As many children as possible were to take part in this magnificent undertaking, so you can imagine how many shepherds, lambs, and angels were cast.

One of the boys suggested they write in an extra stop for Mary and Joseph, so he could be the last innkeeper, but Gretchen was not amused. The story had to be told the right way and that was all there was to it. She was not so secretly hoping she would be chosen to be Mary, one of the parts not yet assigned.

When she thought no one was looking, she would practice what she thought was serene, Mary-like behavior. She no longer walked. She glided. She "Yes, Mother"-ed and "No, Mother"-ed me until I was ready to scream. One day I came upon her with my pashmina on. It did look a little like a veil.

Poor Paul, her dad, missed his little wrestling buddy. Gretchen was no longer interested in horsing around with him. Her mind was on more spiritual matters. We began to, collectively, hold our breath, hoping she wouldn't be too disappointed if someone else were chosen.

On THE day, our little saint demurely went off with the rest of the kids in her car pool, her hair NOT in braids. "So, Sister Pat can see how long it is, Mom, like Mary's…" Never did CCD take so long. I waited by the front door until the car pulled up and Gretchen got out, then I scurried back to the kitchen.

The front door was slammed shut with more force than necessary, not a good sign. The glide was gone from her step. Her taffy-colored hair was sticking out in all directions, and her eyes were suspiciously shiny.

Three carrots later, she told me she was going to be an angel. "An angel," she snorted in disgust. "Everybody's an angel." To make matters worse, one of her friends had been chosen to be Mary. "She'll be a terrible Mary, Mom. She has short hair and everything."

A very sad girl dragged herself upstairs to her room where she wallowed in self-pity the rest of the afternoon. When Paul came home that night, Gretchen met him at the door.

"Hi, Dad," she said. "Wanna wrestle?"

A Love Story

When Paul and I moved our little family to upstate New York, the kids were thrilled. They loved our new house. They loved its second story deck. They loved its laundry chute. And they loved playing with their new baby, three-month old Stephanie, whom they somehow thought came with the house.

The Deck

Jim had a Steve Austin (The Bionic Man) action figure and Gretchen had a Barbie. They would raid Paul's handkerchief drawer, tie handkerchief parachutes to their dolls' hands, and then throw them off the deck. Amazingly, sometimes the "chutes" would open and the dolls would have a safe landing. When this didn't happen and the dolls crashed, the children would set up a triage area and bandage broken doll limbs, now a gory red with ketchup blood.

The Laundry Chute

Their focus then shifted to the laundry chute. They would open its 12" by 12" door and drop their long-suffering dolls down. This was usually an attempt to have the dolls land either in, or on, the laundry basket stoically waiting three floors below.

The New Baby

When we moved, Jim was four and a half years old, and Gretchen was three. They loved another new game they made up called "slide the baby." Sitting two feet apart, legs spread in a "V," they would slide Stephanie, in her thickly padded sleep sac, back and forth to each other. Steph, cooing and smiling, seemed to enjoy the fun.

I should have figured that the next really great idea would involve two out of three of their favorites...I was upstairs vacuuming when something made me stop to check on the kids. There was Jim trying to stuff his three-month old sister down the laundry chute. I grabbed her and looked down, down, down. Gretchen, three stories below, was waiting, her arms raised, ready to catch the baby.

We lived in Fairport, NY, for four years. Somehow, Stephanie survived.

Jim, now in his forties, is *still* really great at making up games. Gretchen, also in her forties, is *still* always up for the next crazy one. Steph, who adores them both, won't let her kids play with Uncle Jim or Aunt Gretchen unless she is nearby.

Imagine.

The Stairs

When Steph, the youngest of our three kids, began nursery school, it was in Mountain Lakes, New Jersey. We had just moved, and I was not familiar with the traditions and rules of the school there. Still, I wasn't worried. Time, I figured, would take care of all of this.

Steph loved school. She was always telling tales of school happenings. She knew all the songs, all the names of the naughty boys (whose exploits she described with the half shocked, half admiring tones of a good little girl), and all the news about her teachers. "Mrs. Elliott got a ticket for speeding. She said the same word Daddy said when he hurted his toe on the ironing board. You 'member that word, Mom?"

One of Steph's especially positive feelings about school seemed to be centered on the school stairs. She would clamber into the car with her chubby little legs sticking straight out and proudly tell me she got to sit on the stairs again today. With a new home and two other children to get settled, I somehow let the clarification of the 'school step mystery' elude me. Steph was happy. I wasn't greedy.

When Steph began first grade, I got a part-time job at her (nursery school) alma mater. As general factotum, I soon learned the survival rules indigenous to nursery school life.

School policy ruled that good behavior be positively reinforced through warm words of praise, stars, stickers, and hugs. Poor manners were discouraged through firm words of rebuke, perhaps a period of time during which a specific toy was off limits, and a hug that made clear that the child was loved even if his behavior was not.

The very naughty child was severely punished by being banished to the stairs.

A Funny Thing Happened on the Way to the Emergency Room

We got very silly one night at the dinner table. Jim started it. He began by saying how much he hated the IV they put in his hand before his arthroscopic surgery. He was afraid to move once it was in place for fear he would make an air bubble that would go to his brain. He said he was lying there trying not to even breathe when the orderly came in to shave his knee. The man moved Jim's hand out of the way and sure enough Jim watched a bubble work its way up the tube. He called to Paul and in a hoarse voice told him, "Dad, if I go into a coma, pull the plug..." We laughed at the way Jim told us the story, but he must have been really scared at the time.

Then Paul chimed in with his favorite hospital story. When his appendix ruptured, peritonitis set in and he was very sick. He looked like he was wired for sound, with tubes and drains and monitoring machines making weird noises all around him. One morning, the monitor that normally went "blip...blip...blip..." went "eeeeeeeeeeee." Paul thought his body had died and his brain was still alive. The nurse came running in and punched the unit on the wall.

"Don't worry about that, Mr. Garstka," she said. "It keeps going off like that; it's not you. It's the machine."

The first time he was allowed out of bed, Paul fixed it.

My experience came when Gretchen had to have her adenoids removed. "A very simple procedure that should take half an hour at the most," the doctor said. He also said he would call me as soon as everything was over. I waited for his call for three hours. I paced and read and paced and paced and paced. When I couldn't take the waiting any more, I stormed to the nurses' station and demanded information about my daughter.

"Why, Mrs. Garstka, they're bringing her up now," the surprised nurse informed me. Apparently, everything had gone well. The doctor had been unable to reach me because I had been waiting in the wrong room.

As a family, we have had our share of medical traumas. But something very positive has come about as a direct result of them. There is nothing like the sight of siblings in pain to remind one they aren't so bad after all. Steph and Gretchen fight like cats and dogs, but when Gretchen broke her leg, it was Steph who was her willing slave. And when Steph fell out of the tree and damaged her kidney, Gretchen was a wreck for weeks.

I'm certainly not going to say I'm glad we broke all those bones or had all those operations or that I enjoyed the hours in the emergency room. But to appreciate good health or to be empathetic towards those who do not have it, one has to have been there. And we have.

Teen Gretchen

A lot of times writing to you is as easy as writing the family letters home. Today hasn't been one of those days. I've been down for a while over the situation between Gretchen and me. We're so alike; we've always had a special ease with each other. But lately that has changed. She's not only growing up, she's growing away from me, and I can't seem to bridge the gap.

I've made a lot of jokes about letting go, and until now I've been able to see the lighter side of the "terrible teens," but lately the healing gift of laughter seems to have vanished from my ken.

Part of my problem is the fact that I have no precedent to fall back on. I didn't fight with my mom. It could have been because I had plenty of others to duke it out with, but I like to think it was because we were so close, it was never necessary.

It's hard for our kids to realize that, as parents, we are learning on the job as it were. When we are strict, it's because we care, not because we lack trust. When we punish them, it is with a value lesson in mind, not because we get our kicks by being mean. And when they lash out at us, we can be hurt.

I know things will come full circle. I look forward to the friendship Gretchen and I will have as two adult women. But for now, I ache for what was.

Inchworm

"Inchworm, inchworm, measuring the Marigolds
You and your arithmetic you'll probably go far.
Inchworm, inchworm, measuring the Marigolds
Seems to me you'd stop and see how beautiful they are."
Frank Loesser

One day, the kids took me school shopping. Jim bought pants made from the black parachutes used by the Green Berets during their night raids. Gretchen bought ankle socks that were bright orange and bright green and proceeded to wear one green one and one orange one as a matched pair. Steph got a mini skirt.

Was I upset by their choices? Not at all. I was just surprised with maybe a little chagrin?

When had Steph gotten tall enough to carry off a mini-skirt? I could swear that last night she was just a little kid. And two odd socks, glow-in-the-dark yet! When had Gretchen gotten enough self-confidence to be that different? And Jim, the last bastion of preppiness, my button-down kid, trying a new approach?

Where was I when they were growing, stretching, changing? I think I was gardening, painting the shutters, playing tennis. Boy, does that make me mad! I was going to be there. I was going to be one of the aware mothers who marveled at each nuance of growth. Instead I was fighting with the kids over important things like whose turn it was to take out the garbage and who left the pack of gum in his jeans and put them in the wash? And why was it my turn to answer the phone? It was going to be for one of them anyway?

I hope the kids haven't cornered the market on growing. It seems I've got some to do myself.

Our Ethical Will

Dear Children,

There are a million things one thinks of when faced with his mortality. The war and living in close proximity to a very desirable target for terrorism has gotten your father's and my brains really humming. For once, he and I agree. Our first concern is for all of you. We couldn't be happier with your choices of life partners or the adults you have become. Our will is prepared, as are we, for the normal end to things. We just have a few concerns about the abnormal.

Our thoughts have become centered more and more on another type of legacy, one of principles and faith. Hopefully you have learned these things, if not through our actions, then through our words. They bear repeating anyway.

Be honest. It works.

Be compassionate. It will make you strong.

Do the complete job.

Be generous with your time and talents. You are all so very gifted and blessed.

Be kind. It is such a little thing with such far-reaching consequences.

Be quiet and let God in.

Save some of your earnings.

Love one another. Family is everything.

Don't fight.

Share.

We love you.

Mom and Dad

Thank you for the music, the songs I'm singin'
Thanks for all the joy they're bringin'
Who can live without it, I ask in all honesty
What would life be, without a song or a dance, what are we?
So, I say, thank you for the music, for giving it to me.
ABBA

Caroline

Our voices were hoarse and exhausted and off-key as we sang "Sweet Caroline" together. We were serenading our four-pound granddaughter, whose appendix had ruptured at birth. Two brand new grandmothers, we each held one tiny preemie foot, the only part of her we were allowed to touch, and sang and wept together.

Caroline, now seventeen years old, insists that our wobbly, sad voices were the reason she got better. She says, "I knew I would have to survive, if only to tell you two never to sing together again." She has a weird sense of humor, and probably got it from her mother's side of the family.

Susan is my son Jim's mother-in-law and my friend. She called Paul and me in New Jersey and told us we should come to Decatur "tonight." Paul and I already had airline tickets to fly to Georgia in six days, and said so. She just repeated, "You should come tonight."

We were there in four and a half hours. Our first grandchild had been born early and her ruptured appendix had gone undiagnosed until her young, frantic, parents had insisted on more tests.

Caroline's weight was down to three and a half pounds when they were told she would need surgery. Our red-eyed, exhausted son Jim embraced us and told us things weren't looking promising. As we waited together, he and Cindy held each other close, quietly weeping.

Susan and I sang to Caroline after her surgery when she was in the NICU (neonatal intensive care unit). Both Cindy and Caroline stayed in the hospital for six weeks. Susan and I visited often, and, as Caroline got better, so did our voices. Well, mine did.

But it was a long road back for their little family.

Each July, Caroline comes north to us, to our new home in Massachusetts, for "Camp Grandma." We swim, ride bikes, cook, shop, and, sometimes, go to Red Sox games. She especially loves it at the games when everyone sings "Sweet Caroline." She seems to think all the voices raised in song are singing for her.

For some reason, so do I.

Time Spent with Grandpa

Tongue clamped between Italian-ice colored lips
Narrowed eyes focused on the prize
Damp tendrils spiking from beneath a ball cap
Safety goggles' elastic splaying first- grader ears
A man's work in a man's workshop
Time spent with Grandpa
Gnarled hands guiding starfish ones
Even, honest, and true, the wood begins to shine
Now a name crookedly soldered on top
V i n c e n t
A boy's first toolbox

Will's Heart

In January of 2012, my daughter-in-law Cindy, a beautiful, vibrant forty-one-year-old, was diagnosed with breast cancer. She met the challenges of this disease the way she faces her everyday life: with grit, intelligence, and humor. And although she spoke openly with her three children, Caroline, Will, and Anna, about cancer and the problems it could entail, Will, her nine-year-old son, seemed to grasp the enormity of their fight and its possible awful conclusion before his sisters did.

That summer on our family vacation Will found a heart-shaped shell on the beach which he showed me. "Do you think this would make a nice necklace for my mom?" he asked.

I thought it would and said so. And the moment passed.

In November, I visited their family in Decatur, Georgia. Cindy was having a third reconstruction surgery, and I wanted to help in any way I could. Cancer takes more than its victims on its long, sad journey.

Will brought the shell out again. This time he was more direct. "Could you make this into a necklace for my mom?" he asked, his eyes direct and intensely blue.

Only a grandchild with immense faith would ask that question of me. Since I had painted and colored and done crafts with him from his toddler days, Will knew I was not an artist. I did, however, have many friends who were. And my quest began with them. In Georgia and in Massachusetts, I asked for help from painters and sculptors, whittlers and quilters. I visited craft stores and gadget stores and art galleries. I went on line. No one wanted to try to make a necklace from such a slender, fragile shell.

Additionally, Will insisted that the chain, or ribbon, holding the shell had to be red. "It's her favorite color," he said.

I was worried. Will believed in me, and I hated to let him down. But I too was afraid of breaking his precious heart.

Then Melissa arrived to visit her mother who was my next door neighbor and friend. A new mother herself, she was charmed by the thought of a son wanting to give his mother such a gift. Additionally,

Melissa's mother had also had cancer, and I think she connected with Will on several different planes. I believe she also relished the challenge of doing the deed. In two days it was finished. By wrapping gossamer wires around the shell, she avoided drilling through it. Triple lines of slender red ribbon made the necklace everything Will had asked for.

The finished necklace arrived in Georgia some two days after I mailed it. In the interim, Will had called me twice and texted me three times asking, "When do you think it will arrive?"..."I did send it to him, not his mom, right?"..."It was padded really good, so it wouldn't break, right?"

I have first-hand accounts of Will's mad runs home from school to check the mail those two days. He took the small bubble-wrap encased package and ran upstairs to his room to open it and to make sure it was not only not broken but also what he had asked for. After all, it was going to be his gift for his mom...

I'm told Cindy, who hadn't cried during any of her cancer treatments, surgeries, and rehabilitation sessions, wept when Will gave her his present. He was, initially, upset that he had made his mom cry, but she assured him they were happy tears.

She wears the necklace on very special occasions. Will beams when she does.

Out of the Mouths of Babes ...

I took my grandchildren to see the Mayflower during their spring break from school. I thought my stories about their ancestors had hit home until I overheard this conversation.

Anna: "*Let's go upstairs and pretend we're our ansisters.*"

Alex: "*And brothers ...*"

*****

While visiting us at the Cape, my daughter Gretchen and her daughters made plans to go to Nantucket. I told one granddaughter, Jessie, that they were going to take the ferry boat there. She disappeared. I, somewhat bemused, returned to my newspaper. She raced back in, fairy wings in hand, and said, "Should I wear my wings, Grandma, or just bring them?"

*****

Our four-year-old granddaughter Anna raced into the kitchen one day and excitedly relayed some brand-new facts she had learned about the weather at preschool...

"Sometimes there is thunder," she began.

"And sometimes there is lightening."

"And, sometimes," – a pause here for effect – "there's a great big tomato!"

*****

It was nighttime, story time, and Jessie and Casey were lying in bed with me, waiting to hear another "Molly Tale." Molly was our beloved Golden Retriever who had died the previous spring. Happily, the little girls focused more on our joyous times together than the dog's illness. They loved to hear all about Molly's early puppy adventures. They also loved to add all the particulars I would carelessly leave out. I had told them so many stories, I struggled to think of one they hadn't heard.

Then, genius struck. They didn't know we had changed Molly's name. They didn't know that Molly's first given name was "Montana." I began, with great drama, to recount the tale of Molly and her original name. When I got to the part where "Montana" was introduced, Casey

116

interrupted me. With both arms held straight out in a "STOP" gesture, she said, "Wait, Grandma, wait. I know what 'Montanas are." She paused a minute to gather her thoughts, then announced. "They're the things that stick up out of a butterfly's head."

Pets: What Were We Thinking?

Killer

**I wrote this story about Killer from another's point of view.
It is narrated by my daughter Gretchen.**

"Hold his head still, Jim. He's making my lines all squiggly." Isn't it funny how an image stays in your mind years after its importance has faded? Killer was our first and only pet. An allergy-ridden family, we had run the gamut of species and types in our efforts to find an animal that wouldn't kill one of us. Because we were such neophytes, we treated him like a member of the family, and so he became one. Our first ritual of acceptance was always to mark the height of the newest friend or neighbor on the frame of the laundry room door. Even now, twenty years later, Killer's height mark still proudly adorns the doorway.

Tiny, yellow, fiercely independent, Killer would hop onto the kitchen table despite my mother's protests, and steal Cheerios from our cereal bowls. We, of course, encouraged him in this wrongdoing. He would also disrupt our homework sessions at the supper table by grabbing our pencils, which were three times his length, and rolling them across the flat surface with his feet. Killer also loved to take walks. We would let him out of his cage and down he would glide to the floor where he would enjoy a daily constitutional. We think Killer thought he was a dog. Actually, he was a yellow parakeet and our hearts' delight.

We were never unkind to him, so Killer grew up thinking he was truly deserving of all the attention we were heaping on him. He and Jim

119

were especially close. They were the only boys in the family, but I would hazard a guess that Jim felt guilty because he and his asthma were the reasons we had never had a dog or a cat.

The kitchen sink was another place Killer considered his. A joyous bather, he loved to jump into my mom's warm soapy dishwater. He would sing and splash and spread happiness and suds all over the place. My sister Steph used to love letting him out of his cage when my father was taking a shower. Killer would swoop onto dad's shoulder and startle him. Dad would yell and startle Killer and there would be wet father and wet bird squawking and yapping. It sure made our school mornings livelier.

Steph, my younger sister, took Killer into school for *Show and Tell* one day. Killer, who had never been shy before, trembled and cowered and would do none of his tricks. From that day, he was a changed bird. Somehow, he picked up a cold he could never quite shake. He was a different bird. Our morning Cheerios ritual no longer appealed to him. Our pencils became too heavy for him to push. Now when Jim held him, Killer would rub his beak on Jim's thumb in a gentle caress instead of his usual pinky nip. A sick parakeet is a cuddly parakeet. Whereas before, Killer would make us coax and wheedle to get him on our fingers, now he would call to us. And when we would open the cage door, he would hop right out. He was always fluffed up as though my mom had put him in the dryer. Then one day, Jim found him on the floor of his cage. Too weak to stay on his perch, he just lay in Jim's palm while Jim stroked his feathers. My mom said he wanted us to say goodbye to him before he went to sleep. So we did and he did.

I'm not sure if Killer was our pet or we were his. Adults now, we laugh and smile when we talk about him. But in all these years and with all the times we've painted my parents' kitchen, Killer's height mark still stands. A giant in our family, he was two and half inches tall.

Samantha

We had a cat. We called her Samantha, 'Sam' for short. She had been ours ever since our daughter Stephanie was told she couldn't keep a cat in her college dorm. Actually, that's not true. After Sam was kicked out of Bates College, she went to Connecticut where she gave both  Grandma and Papa hives. She then had a short stint in Westfield, NJ, where Gretchen resided. This visit, too, was cut short when Gretchen, who lived in an apartment, was told either she or the cat would have to go. To round out this picture, I will mention that Samantha was born in Georgia. Our son, Jim, in an effort to keep his housemates from drowning the litter of kittens born under their porch, rashly promised to find homes for each of them. Samantha then became his Christmas gift for Stephanie.

My husband Paul was not a cat person. This is a statement he made frequently. "Don't like cats, never will." But Sam knew better. She set out to charm him, and he fell like a ton of bricks. In the early morning hours, I would often hear him talking to her as he did his stretches. One morning I came down to find her sitting on his stomach while he was doing sit-ups. He mumbled something about the added weight being better for him, but at the time she weighed less than three pounds.

A napper, she and Paul had that in common. She'd climb up onto his lap and in five minutes the two of them would be fast asleep. Extremely territorial, Sam had to deal with two new cats in our neighborhood. One, a male, decided to serenade her on a nightly basis. The other, a female, had the nerve to come onto our screened-in porch. I opened the door to the house one day and the female went rushing off the porch. I was yelling at her when Sam came next to me hissing and growling. She made it clear that it was she who had vanquished the interloper. Trembling with rage (fear), she stood at the door of the porch and in effect yowled, "And don't come back again!"

Because Sam came to us when our "empty nest" stage of life was beginning, it seemed natural that I check on her each night before I went to bed, the way I always had with our other children. I would pat her downy head and say, "Good night, silly kitten." Over the years, this evolved to the nightly ritual of a hug and the words "Goodnight, silly cat; I love you."

Sam was fourteen years old when we learned she had a thyroid problem. Our vet had some pretty drastic remedies for this, radiation being one, but we demurred. Sam had had a long history with us; we would deal with her symptoms ourselves. And we did. For the most part, we simply fed her much more food, much more often, and gave her more loving attention. She grew thinner but still hung in there three more years.

One night as I was hugging her, she touched my face with her paw. I think she was saying, "Good bye, silly human. I love you, too," because she died that night.

My mind knows this was nature at its best, but my heart is still working on it.

Molly

Molly had been with us three days when she broke her right hind leg. An adorable Golden Retriever puppy, she was even cuter with a pink (for a girl) cast. Puppies grow at an astonishing rate. Soon Molly's cast was exchanged for a splint. A lovely shade of purple, it lasted two days. Then Molly got it caught in some ivy and walked out of it. Back we went to the vet. We figured three visits in thirteen days had to be some kind of a record.

But wait, there's more. Not only did Molly get a new splint, royal blue this time, she also got an Elizabethan collar. They look like large

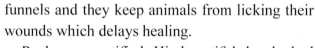 funnels and they keep animals from licking their wounds which delays healing.

Paul was mortified. His beautiful dog looked pathetic and ridiculous. And the neighbors had a field day ribbing him.

We went to Puppy Kindergarten next. Miss Molly was a star in obstacle courses, sitting, and taking the good dogs' rewards away from them.

She got low marks for not coming, not staying, not listening, and for taking the good dogs' rewards away from them. The teacher suggested Miss Molly go on for higher learning, but Paul and I thought not.

A young lady now, Molly has a beau. His name is Miles, and he lives three houses away. The two of them run and play and jump and chase each other. Miles visits Molly, and Molly visits Miles. Both families used to have wonderful lawns. Now they have wonderful dogs and lawns that look terrible.

Jim and Cindy and Gretchen and Steph gave us Molly for our anniversary. She has been a terrific gift. Paul thinks she guards me when he is traveling. Molly thinks I'm guarding her when Paul is traveling. Sam, the cat, thinks she could take Molly in a fight. Molly thinks Sam could take her in a fight. I think our vet is having us investigated.

Life is good.

Annie

"I've done something impulsive." Paul was calling home from work before he left for the night.

"Good for you!" I interjected cheerfully. My husband, a type-A personality if ever there was one, is also a corporate controller, which leaves little to no room for impulsive behavior. "What did you do?"

"I got us another dog," he replied. "She's one of the Spaniels from the company's hunting lodge. The trainer told me she wasn't going to make it, so I told him I'd take her. She's a real sweetie. You'll love her."

He was right. The first time I saw Annie, I thought she was perhaps the homeliest animal I'd ever seen. A skinny, scrawny little thing with ears too big for her puppy face, she walked into our house and our hearts and took over.

She asked our other dog, Molly, a Golden Retriever, the following questions:

"Who used to be in charge?" When Molly told her that the boss was a cat named Sam, Annie nearly laughed her puppy head off. "Do cats taste good?" she asked.

To Annie's question of what do we drink? Molly said they would probably be drinking Paul's left-over cereal milk and water. Annie chuckled. "I prefer coffee, mostly black," she said. "I'll just drink theirs; they won't even notice."

Then she asked Molly, "Where do we sleep?" When Molly told her "We sleep on our beds downstairs," Annie snorted. "I like sofas and chairs," she said.

I asked Paul. "What were we thinking?"

He answered, "I haven't a clue. Did you drink my coffee?"

Bridget and Me

Bridget and I are starting to show our age. She is seventy in dog years, and I am more than that in human years. When we overdo things, we pay. She has doggy arthritis. I have a new knee.

If we take too long a hike, we both limp our way back to the car.

If we're going to sit on the floor, we both let out an *oooff* as we land.

If we watch TV, from the floor, we both struggle to get back up. *Downward Dog* has become much more than a yoga pose to me. And, I'll admit it: It annoys me that she's better at it than I am. Can't think why.

Her fur is still thick and pretty, but her muzzle is turning white. My hair? Let's not go there.

We both love Good & Plenty candy. One day I spilled a few. They rolled from the kitchen island to the floor and Bridget pounced on them. Now I have to sneak my Good & Plenty candy when she's outside. If I get careless, or forget, her *Spidy-senses* hear the candies rattling in the box and she comes running.

Five winters ago, I fractured my tibia while jogging on the golf course. She ran over to me, and then, like Lassie, went to get help. Actually, Bridget doesn't know a thing about Lassie or the proper way for a dog to get help. She gave me a "Gee that looks nasty" glance and went back to her normal routine of sniffing every rock, shrub, and tree in her doggy world. I hobbled back to the car by myself.

One thing she has taught me is that unconditional love does exist.

If I bathe her, after she has had a heavenly roll in coyote scat; even if I wash away its deliciously foul lingering odor, she still loves me. I'm guessing that might be because she has memorized the location of the coyote's toilet and has plans to return.

✱ Bridget loves her stuffed animal babies. She rips them apart, chews on their faces, and then spits their eyes out. Our front yard looks like a Zombie-Dog land, with eye-less stuffed toys and their vacant, staring eyes all over the place. Paul freaks out when he mows the lawn and glassy eyes go flying.

✱ NOTE: WE STOPPED buying STUFFED TOYS WITH EYES. NOW BUY THE ONES WITH EMBROIDERED ONES. ⌣

I no longer know what it is to eat a meal or a snack without a drooling canine audience. I don't mind the drooling; it's the sharing I resent. I don't even share food with Paul. I learned to be miserly with my meals from years of dining with the lightning fast forks of four brothers.

Shoestrings? Bridget loves them. If she's sitting under the desk while I'm at the computer, she's using her teeth and paws to hold my foot down and to untie my double-knotted shoelaces. According to her, aglets are the best part, with grommets a close second. She breaks them down, spits them out, and then grins at me.

She hates it when I wear loafers.

When Bridget developed some hearing issues, I worked with a trainer on signals that she can easily see and understand. Sometimes though, she just can't be bothered to obey. I'll give her the sign to *come* and she will, literally, cup her ear with her right front paw and mime the words, "I can't hear; don't you remember?"

Bridget loves my stories, even the ones she has heard a thousand times. She may live five more years; she may live two. I'm just grateful for the time we have had together. And, if there is a heaven, she will be waiting for me, and my shoelaces, and my stories, and my Good & Plenty candies, and for stuffed toys with eyes.

In My Opinion

An Open Letter About Friendship, Our Daughters, and Abortion

Dear Jane,

Twenty years ago, when you asked me what did I think about abortion, we seemed to be on the same page. I said I could never have one but that my daughters felt differently. And that I would try to support their choice as best I could should one need to be made.

At no time in their teen years, or later, did I suggest that abortion was the answer to their problems. What I did do was tell them if they thought they were mature enough to be sexually active, then they were mature enough to prevent an unwanted pregnancy. And I took them to see a gynecologist.

I know your daughter had an abortion when she was in high school. I also know her well enough to know she did not make that decision lightly. She had always been a warm, bright, loving and loyal girl. She was never afraid of hard work (witness the hundreds of five-thirty mornings when she tended the horses), so it was not the idea of the work a child would entail that made the decision for her. We'll never really know what her deciding moment was. What we do know, and did know, was that it was not our choice to make.

I know you feel I am critical of the Christian Right. I am. I am also critical of my own Catholic Church. It seems to me that these "Christians" are terribly unforgiving, unyielding, and unloving. Not exactly what Christ advocated.

I would also like to get away from the stereotypical description of the average individual seeking an abortion. There is no average. They are not all teenage girls who are "sluts and whores." They are the woman whose husband is out of work, the addict who can't live her own life much less guide the life of a child; they are the women with six kids who just can't nurture another one. And, globally, they are the women whose society sees them as less than able to have any say about their lives or their bodies.

Respect life isn't only about the unborn child. It's about the life of the children already born, and it's about the life of their mother. We don't have the right to make a woman have a baby *we want*. We won't be there 24/7 to help her love and nurture and feed and clothe and educate the child, so we don't have the right to make it happen and then walk away feeling we did our duty before the Lord.

Which brings me back to you, Jane. I have always admired you. You were and are a fabulous mother. You gave your children love, scruples, attention, a strong work ethic, and again love. Your daughter's decision was made twenty years ago. Don't you think it's time to let go of your perceived guilt and move on? It wasn't your fault. It wasn't your decision. It was your daughter who had the courage to decide, for herself, in a time that was not an accepting one.

When you asked me the question, "What do you think about abortion?" I already loved your child. After you told me of her decision, I still loved her. You raised a strong woman and a good one. She's a lot like her mother.

An Open Letter About Golf from Your Mother

All right, all right, I may not be *your* mother, but I'm here to remind you of some of the things I'm positive she taught you.

1. Clean up after yourself.
2. Put the caps back on your empty water bottles then discard them in the proper receptacles.
3. If you're old enough to smoke a cigar, you are old enough to field strip it and not leave your stogie on the course.
4. Nips are fun. If you're old enough to drink them, you should be old enough to toss the empties in the garbage.
5. Red Bull cans, beer cans, iced tea bottles, and granola bar wrappers – no matter your age or gender, see #3 and #4.
6. The sport of golf has many courtesies embedded in its rules. For example, being quiet while someone is putting is a no brainer.
7. So, let's talk about courtesy on the course itself. When a bottle or wrapper or nip falls out of your cart, stop to retrieve it.
8. Ball markers and tees, only bring enough so that you would notice that six or seven have fallen out of your pocket or golf bag.
9. Golf is an expensive sport. I know you have worked hard to get to the point where you can play it. But your sense of entitlement, has you essentially trashing your own back yard.
10. Respect the course property so its beauty and serenity are maintained.

When I walk my Golden Retrieve in the early morning hours, I pick up her poop. I also see and pick up many of the things you have left behind. Whether you meant to or not isn't the point. Being aware of your physical and mental game is an important part of golf. Maybe being aware that you could do better in this one area, could help you in another.

Remember: I love you and I'm telling you this for your own good.

"Alas for Those Who Never Sing, But Die with All Their Music in Them."
Oliver Wendell Holmes, Sr.

My parents were always quoting wiser and better educated people in order to teach us stuff. Most times, they, the quotations, went right over our pointed little heads, but that never stopped Mom and Dad from trying.

One time Sandie and I were fighting over something important; I'm pretty sure it was a hairbrush. I guess our yelling alerted mom to the argument because she walked into our room, said, "See those Christians, how they love one another" and walked out. Neither Sandie nor I got her point, but we stopped wrestling, which was probably all Mom wanted.

Another of Mom's favorites was, "Alas for those who never sing, but die with all their music in them." This one was a little easier to understand, but it still took us a while to grasp. Teens, preteens, and small children, we took things too literally to understand its deeper meaning until later, much later.

We were all introduced to music at an early age, some of us with better results than others. Puss had a clear, true, strong, soprano voice. Joe, on the other hand, couldn't carry a tune with a wagon. Like our dad, Moe had been a boy soprano. When Moe's voice changed, he became a baritone; I have no idea how that happened. I thought a boy soprano would automatically become a tenor. Moe was also able to play the piano "by ear." This annoyed, to no end, those of my siblings who had to plow through weekly practices and lessons with Mrs. Laurie, a brilliant music teacher who always had onion breath.

I took the mandolin.

Puss, Gin, Gret, Sandie, Pat, and I were "the chorus." Harmony was easy for us because we were so attuned to each other's voices. We sang while we did the dishes. We sang while we folded laundry. We sang when we rode our bikes. That scene in *The Sound Of Music*...Maria and the Von Trapp children probably got that idea from us.

Mike joined the grammar school band when he was in fourth grade. One day he came home from practice to announce that his music teacher had made him *Chairman of the Band*. Needless to say, our Mom was pleased, until she found out it meant Mike set up all the chairs for the band rehearsals.

When Chris was five, he was naughty. He was told he would have to "face the music;" so he walked over to Mom's piano and stood in front of it.

Sometimes I feel bad that my children don't sing together. Music in my/our family became more of a spectator sport with the fine-tuning of TVs, radios, and stereos, which had better sounds and better singers. My siblings and I still sing whenever we get together, but my kids do not. They're much too busy being embarrassed and getting more wine.

My children also still can't get their heads around the fact that, when we were kids, three or four of us would lie beneath our mom's concert grand piano to listen to her play.

When I graduated from eighth grade, my mom signed my yearbook. She wrote:

Don't be ♯ (sharp)

Don't be ♭ (flat)

Just be ♮ (natural)

I got that one because by then I was thirteen: wiser, better educated, and I played the mandolin.

Costumes

In my time as a mom-at-home, I was able to don many a unique disguise. In fact, I wore so many, Paul thought I had the ulterior motive of scaring the children away.

In chronological order, I was Mrs. Santa Claus, the Easter Bunny, Sister Mary Nut -Job, a Clown Hobo, and a Wicked Witch.

The regular Mrs. Santa Claus was sick, and I was asked, at the eleventh hour, to fill in for her at our church's *Breakfast With Santa*. Her costume was perfect. My small problem was that I didn't fill it out as well as she did. My neighbor Tom, who was a rep for a medical supplier, took one look at me and said, "Wait here. I have the perfect thing." He ran home, which was next door, and returned with two gel breast implants. He began to insert one into my costume, when his wife intervened.

"I'll do it," she said with some exasperation. The implants were a great success because the babies I was caring for fell asleep as soon as they rested their little heads against my (now) marvelous chest.

Being the Easter Bunny was a different gig altogether. I was given cash to rent the full costume. The town egg hunt was scheduled for a Saturday, so my best friend and I rented the *rabbit regalia* on Friday. We then visited two elementary schools in the area and gave out Tootsie Roll Pops. One kindergartener grabbed my tail and told everyone, "Yep, it's the Easter Bunny alright. I can tell cause his tail is furry."

Sister Mary Nut-Job was my role in our town's follies. A fundraiser for our schools, the Follies snared nearly everyone in town. Because it was *for the kids,* one was either on stage or donating time, money, or sweat equity. I was in an act that featured the song "Kids" from the show *Bye Bye Birdie*. I was the only nun because I had the costume. We sang, "Kids, who can tell what's wrong with these kids today…" We were amazingly good. Well, I was.

As one of the PTA officers, my job was to hold hands with first and second graders in the school Halloween Parade. I was dressed as a pretty scary clown hobo. I was a little worried that I might frighten my charges. But that was not the case. One of my daughter Stephanie's classmates whispered, "Did you bring us any cookies, Mrs. G?"

So much for my Academy Award winning bad guy act.

My Wicked Witch appearance was the brilliant idea of my kids' dentist. He was sponsoring a booth at a fair/fundraiser for St. Clare's, our local hospital. I was hunched over, my teeth blackened, wearing a gauzy black wig, a pointy witch hat and nose. Brandishing a huge toothbrush, I was to say. "Kids, eat candy and some day your teeth will look like mine." I was really getting into my role, overacting, when there was a tap on my shoulder. I turned to face one of my former college roommates. She said, "Jonnie, is that you? I thought so."

I hadn't seen her in twenty years and she recognized me as a witch?

Hmm…maybe I wasn't as nice a roomie as I thought I was.

Because our town was so small, I was involved in a lot of activities. I enjoyed them all, but I had the most fun wearing disguises.

Well, it was fun for me.

For my kids, not so much.

Bet You a Nickel

I once heard my Uncle Hans say that my brother Chris was "married from the day he was born." At the time, I didn't know just what he meant, but now I do.

Chris grew up with six older sisters who were more than happy to tell him everything he was doing wrong and how to change the way he was doing things for the better.

We nagged him mercilessly for everything from his thumb sucking to his "being a baby," which he was in actual number of years.

Potty training him was easy. And, although he trained quite early, can't think why, he would often forget to re-zip his pant's zipper. We'd say, "Zip it, Chris," and, "Shut the barn door, Chris," to no avail.

One day, when I told him, yet again, that his fly was open, he said, "No, it isn't."

I said, "Yes, it is."

He said, "No, it isn't. Bet you a nickel."

I won that bet and the vast sum of five cents which, in itself, was not a big deal. What was a big deal, however, was the way my family embraced his phrase, *Bet you a nickel*. It became our *go-to code* for anything in or on our clothing that needed to be adjusted, closed, tugged down, hoisted up, or repaired.

It worked then and does now. We can alert each other with no one else knowing there is an issue. For instance, not too long ago, four of my sisters and I shared a cabin in the Georgia Mountains. We decided to tease Ginger, who is easily the nicest and most gullible person in the family. When she entered the cabin's sun porch, we four said, in unison, "Bet you a nickel." She began to frantically paw at her clothing, looking for the problem.

There wasn't one. We were just messing with her. It was fun, but it would have been more fun messing with Chris.

My Sermon Would Be Better ...

Sometimes I sit in church and think, modestly, "I could give a better sermon than this." Frustrated by how often priests seem to need a better connection to or a greater empathy for their captive audiences, I have begun to mentally fix the problem. For example, when there are a lot of children at a particular Mass, I would try to make the lesson more interesting.

Take the twenty-third psalm and all the Biblical references to shepherds, *please*. A church located on the South Shore of Massachusetts, in the USA would most likely have parishioners whose idea of a shepherd is commensurate with the European method of tending sheep. I speak of Border Collies nipping at the heels of stupid, bewildered ovine.

I actually have a friend who said she resented the idea of something nipping at her feet, faith-wise, corralling her, forcing her to take a specific path ...

This is such an easy fix. In the Near East, shepherds gather together in the evening for the safety of their flocks. There could be a thousand sheep grouped together. Come morning, when it is time to leave, the first shepherd rises and begins to sing as he walks away. His sheep know his voice and they follow him. "I know mine and mine know me." The relationship in this situation is one of familiarity, love, and trust. Simply explaining this custom would make a great beginning for a sermon.

And, sometimes, the best lesson is no lesson.

One mid-summer's Sunday in the 1970s, when temperatures were in the nineties, our church's air conditioning system broke down. At sermon time, Father McKenna walked to the pulpit. He solemnly intoned, "He that will learn to pray, let him go to the sea," and then he sat down again. I loved Father McKenna. We all did. He gave great sermons.

Ski Lesson

We lived in Rochester, New York for four years. As most people know, there are only two seasons there: winter and the Fourth of July. Young parents of three children under five, Paul and I actually thought going out at night to get ski lessons would be fun. The wind chill of ten degrees did not deter us. We had a babysitter and the lessons were paid for.

Skiing in the Northeast is mostly done on ice and rock. Consequently, one's initial foray into the sport there is a cautionary one. We were taught how to sideslip down a path beyond our skill level, how to traverse large ice lakes on a slope, and how to use our pole tips to chip off any ice that inserted itself between our boots and our bindings.

I was having trouble with my bindings. They were releasing every time I took a turn. The third time they let go, I waved my class on and began to chip away at the ice now clinging to the bottom of my boot. I would plant one pole in the snow, and chip away at the ice with the other.

My "planted pole" danced down the hill away from me. The snow was too icy to hold it in place. I side slipped after it and began, again, the ritual of removing the ice from my boot. The third time it skittered away, I grabbed the runaway pole and, exasperated, put it crossways, in my mouth.

Anyone who ever took a bet to lick an iron fence in the winter, can tell you what came next. My lips froze onto the metal part of the pole.

Side slipping, this time to get down to the lodge. I was greeted with smiles, whistles, and cheerful waves. Mortified, finally, at the bottom of the hill, I threw my skis to the ground and walked sideways into the lodge and again, sideways, into the ladies room.

A kind woman there gestured to me to come over to the hand dryer, which she turned up toward my face. A minute later, I was free. When I emerged from "the ladies," a small but empathetic crowd had gathered. A large man with ice dripping from his beard handed me a steaming cup of hot chocolate. Others patted my shoulder and murmured things like, "It gets better" and "Good for you." No one guffawed, at least within my hearing, except for Paul.

"The City"

When Paul and I moved to Fairport, NY, we were the poor, but proud, parents of three small children. We had a new home with a hefty mortgage and one car.

Jim and Gretchen were each in a preschool that allowed parents to work off their offspring's tuition by being aides and general factotums. Needless to say, my children went to nursery school for free.

I was a stay-at-home-mommy and loved it until the day came when I needed to get away for a bit.

My neighbors suggested that we women do a shopping trip to *The City*. I asked Paul if we could manage a weekend off for me, financially and babysitting-wise, and he said, "Go for it."

Having recently moved to upstate New York from New Jersey, I assumed *The City* meant New York. No, it meant Rochester, which was ten miles away and did not require an overnight bag.

We had a great time.

Fast forward fifteen years and my more affluent lady tennis buddies suggested I join them for a shopping trip to *The City*. One would think I had learned my lesson, but I had not.

Again, Paul said, "Go for it." And I happily prepared for my long-awaited overnight in Manhattan. **BAAP!** Wrong answer. *The City* Laura and Barbara were talking about was Paris, with another quick jaunt to Barbara's family home in Stockholm.

I'm still shaking my head over that one. Although I played tennis often with those kind women, in no way did my clothing or demeanor share their easy comfortable use of large amounts of money.

I blame my mother. She made me learn language and music and literature and manners. Obviously, my friends thought, like them, I had been "to the manor born."

BAAP! Wrong answer.

Ecclesiastic Old Boys Club

There was a great hue and cry, and rightly so, when a senate meeting on women's health issues did not have any women as participants. Yet, when the synod of American Catholic Bishops sent out its letter excoriating the law which calls for insurance coverage for, among other things, women's birth control, the silence was deafening. Why?

The Roman Catholic Church is superbly served by its female congregants. They run programs, teach church doctrine to children from grades one through ten, cook and deliver meals to those in need, man and run thrift shops as businesses, organize health clinics and exercise classes for seniors and volunteer as lectors and Eucharistic Ministers. In some parishes they still vacuum the church and iron the altar linens.

Yet there are no women in the church's hierarchy of authority. (deacons, priests, bishops, etc.) Given this lack of respect for women, and their life experience in the church's structure and councils, I find it hard to accept an edict damning women's medical coverage from an ecclesiastic "Old Boys Club."

How can a group of celibate, middle-aged men determine what is real and difficult and true about limiting, raising, nurturing, and educating a family?

Sadly, the answer is they can't.

The Ovation

At our local Back to School Night, a special education teacher was asked to show us parents how difficult a simple task can be for a child with special needs.

He asked for a volunteer. Mr. Brown, a school board member, cheerfully raised his hand.

While Mr. Brown climbed the stairs to the stage, the teacher showed the audience a five-point star printed on an 8 by 10-inch piece of paper, a magic marker, and a mirror.

"Your job," he said to the board member, "is to outline the star and color it in. Do you think you can do this?"

Mr. Brown confidently replied, "Yes, I'm pretty sure I can." His humorous response drew some laughter from the audience.

The teacher smiled gently and continued.

"Take the mirror in your dominant hand and the marker in your other hand.

Now, looking at the image through the mirror, and using only the mirror, you may begin to edge and then color in the star."

Mr. Brown began and was immediately outside the lines. His marker was all over the page, and nowhere near the star he was supposed to be coloring in.

Next the teacher began to push him.

"Mr. Brown, the others in the class are nearly finished. Can't you go a little faster?" (and) "Mr. Brown, why is your work so messy? Why can't your work be like the others?" (and) "Mr. Brown, I'm afraid you will have to finish your assignment after school."

No one was laughing now.

The teacher got a standing ovation.

Thank You

To Andrea who said, "Let's do it."
To my mom who said, "You can do it."
To my siblings who said, "Do it and we'll get even."
To my husband who said, "Go for it."
To each of my kids who said, "Why me?"
To my readers, who believed my side of the story, most of the time.
To Chris, who initially put it all together.

BIOGRAPHY

 Jonnie Garstka is the sixth of ten children, the mother of three, has nine grandchildren, and is married to an only child. Each of these familial situations has given her a wealth of material for her newspaper columns.